THE FOREIGN EXPANSION
OF AMERICAN BANKS

American Branch Banking Abroad

By

CLYDE WILLIAM PHELPS

Professor of Economics and Head of the Department of Economics
and Commerce in the University of Chattanooga

THE RONALD PRESS COMPANY

NEW YORK

INTRODUCTION

Although one of the cardinal elements in banking reform, as advocated prior to the adoption of the Federal Reserve Act, was the establishment of a more adequate supervision of, and service to, the financing of American foreign trade, the 12 years which have elapsed since the act began operation have seen only a limited progress in this direction. It is strange, but true, that this limited development should have been contemporaneous with the greatest expansion in foreign trade in the history of the United States. This is to be explained, no doubt, by the continuance of the World War during the formative period of the Federal Reserve System but that, after all, would furnish only an explanation of conditions during the years prior to 1919. Our greatest genuine trade expansion has occurred since that time, and it should normally have been accomplished with the assistance and cooperation of American banks. For such cooperation by them the Federal Reserve Act, and its numerous amendments, laid an ample foundation.

And yet the subject still remains very largely a matter for discussion, a field in which opposition is to be overcome and progress secured through argument and the slow growth of conviction. Antagonism on the part of many of the larger American banks has prevented the Federal Reserve Banks from developing the foreign field as they had been expected to do, while fear of losing money or of having to act as pioneers in a doubtful enterprise has kept some of these larger institutions from pressing actively forward with the creation of branch banks abroad.

It must be admitted that the unfavorable experience gained by some American banks which hastily went into foreign countries during the years 1919 and 1920 with their branches seemed to afford a warning against expansion of this kind. A calmer survey of the situation shows that the results of a hasty and inexpertly managed experiment during years of great inflation and deflation can hardly be taken as good ground upon which to base a permanent policy. This fact is being more and more clearly understood and it may be assumed that, as time goes on, American banks will come gradually back into the foreign field and will develop it more systematically as well as more successfully than heretofore.

For this kind of thoughtful and intensive development Professor Phelps' book furnishes an excellent background. He has analyzed more carefully than anyone else both the general structure of foreign connections which is at present maintained by American banks, and also the legal problems which they must confront when they attempt to organize institutions upon foreign soil. He has also given frank consideration to a subject which has been too often overlooked or ignored by former writers—the obstacles that naturally grow out of our own attitude toward, and discrimination against, foreign branch banks. His book thus constitutes both an excellent account of what has been done, an analysis of what may be accomplished by foreign branches and also a study of those problems of public and national policy which must be dealt with if we are to make any real progress in giving banking support to foreign trade in the future.

It is natural that Professor Phelps in this review of the situation should have become strongly impressed with the benefits to be derived from proper organization of foreign branch banking. His studies have shown him that it is through "team-work" by business men and bankers that foreign trade is definitely advanced. This kind of team-work has in fact been the essential basis upon which the success of foreign countries in developing their trade has rested. And so, he naturally argues that Americans should follow the lines which have been mapped out by the experience of others as leading to success, and that their action in so doing will tend to promote here, as it has abroad, the welfare of our national enterprises. He very properly finds one reason for failures heretofore in the haste with which the movement was initiated and the lack of a wisely selected personnel. And yet he recognizes, as have others, that in spite of this apparently unsatisfactory experience a good deal of real progress has been made and valuable lessons learned. He offers no explanation of the failure of reserve banks to go further, although he notes the unfavorable attitude of the American Bankers Association and of the larger commercial banks to broader activity on their part. The reader will be able to draw, as he should, his own conclusions.

The future of our foreign trade will be intimately bound up with our banking policy and will be most directly concerned with the growth and development of our foreign banking. We shall find, as other nations have found, that satisfactory foreign connections are essential and that these are best provided by the efforts of our own banks. In all probability, we shall find ourselves driven eventually to take advantage of the means afforded by our Federal Reserve System, and we shall recognize that the assistance of Federal Reserve Banks will be a furtherance, not an impediment, to the success of our larger commercial institutions in expanding their growth abroad. It will not be long before this subject will present itself with such urgency that the definite action which has thus far been postponed through factious opposition will have to be taken.

On all this controversial side of the discussion Professor Phelps necessarily says little. His statement is, indeed, particularly serviceable in that it is a non-partisan survey of experience, a scientific exposition of facts and conditions covering foreign branch banking. The reader will, however, obtain from it not only knowledge of what has taken place, but the data that he needs in making up his mind with regard to our future banking policy. His work is therefore to be commended to all who have at heart the steady growth of our foreign trade and the retention of our control over it through appropriate financial methods.

H. PARKER WILLIS

Columbia University,
December, 1926.

AUTHOR'S PREFACE

After publishing in Paris a short study on "Les Banques Américaines à l'Étranger et Principalement en France," the writer returned to the United States in 1924 to find that with the exception of a few brief articles in the reviews no treatment of the foreign expansion of American banks had appeared. Perhaps the most interesting developments in American banking since the establishment of the Federal Reserve System have been the trend of federal reserve policy, the growth of the discount market, the increase in banking facilities for agriculture, the movement toward domestic branch banking, and the foreign expansion of American banks. Books have appeared upon all but the last subject, and the present study is an attempt to present the outlines of this interesting phase of American banking.

The foreign expansion of a nation's banks is bound up with the extension of its foreign trade, and consequently the commercial banks have been the principal ones to expand abroad. Before the World War the banks of the great European nations had made a notable foreign expansion in the establishment and acquisition of banking houses all over the world. The foreign expansion of American banks had been slight, due to obstacles both legal and economic in nature, but the passage of the Federal Reserve Act and the World War, with its stimulation of American foreign trade and reversal of the debtor position of the United States, resulted in a striking expansion.

In the past, most of what has been written and said on the subject of American foreign banking expansion has been in the nature of an argument for or against the proposition,

Resolved: that American banking institutions in foreign countries are *necessary* for the development of our foreign trade. The discussion has been interesting, but it seems to the writer that it is time to shove the debaters and their question into the background and consider what has actually been accomplished while the debate was going on. The present work, thus, is not a theoretical argument for or against the proposal that American banks should engage in foreign expansion for the salvation of our foreign commerce, but a description of the foreign expansion already made by American banks.

What kinds of banks and which American banks have engaged in foreign expansion? What methods of expansion have been used and why? What is the extent of the expansion which has taken place? What was the nature of American banking legislation before 1914, and what were its effects upon American foreign banking facilities? What important changes were made by the Federal Reserve Act? What is the legal situation of our banks abroad and of foreign banks in the United States? These are some of the questions to which the writer has endeavored to suggest answers.

This study is limited for the most part to an external treatment of the foreign expansion of American banks. It would be interesting to present the detailed statements of condition of the various American branch banks abroad, to discuss at length the many phases of the situation of each branch, and to treat the practical aspects of branch bank management. These subjects are left for future treatment. In the first attempt at the study of any subject there are always certain omissions to be remedied and corrections to be made, and the writer would welcome criticism to these ends.

I wish to thank Mr. L. M. Jay, vice-president of the International Banking Corporation, Mr. G. B. Sherwell of the Department of Commerce, and Professors O. M. W. Sprague of Harvard, H. P. Willis of Columbia, and G. W. Edwards of New York University, for their kindness in reading and criti-

cising the manuscript.   To Professor A. A. Young of Harvard
I am especially grateful for much helpful criticism and for
valuable suggestions.

CLYDE WILLIAM PHELPS

Chattanooga, Tennessee,
  January 10, 1927.

CONTENTS

THE FOREIGN EXPANSION
OF AMERICAN BANKS

CHAPTER I

INTRODUCTORY

A New Period in American Foreign Banking.—The year 1914 marked the beginning of a new period in the history of American foreign banking. In that year the Federal Reserve Act entered into effect and the World War began. The act contained provisions removing legal obstacles and permitting a free and full expansion of American foreign banking facilities. The war and post-war periods, by greatly stimulating American foreign trade and transforming the United States into a creditor nation, caused a striking expansion of American foreign banking machinery.

Until the passage of the Federal Reserve Act national banks were prohibited from establishing foreign branches and from making acceptances. The private banks and some state banking institutions could exercise these powers but practically no accepting was done by them and but few foreign branches were established. In order to allow the fullest expansion of American foreign banking facilities, federal legislation was demanded to permit national banks to establish branches and to accept, and to provide for the formation of central banks of rediscount which would help to create and maintain a market for American bank acceptances. These demands were satisfied with the passage of the Federal Reserve Act.

But even with the establishment of the federal reserve banks and the removal of the legal obstacles to the fullest expansion of American foreign banking, it is extremely doubtful if any very rapid progress would have been made in the establishment of foreign branch banks or in the creation of a market for American bank acceptances had it not been for the World War. In other words, the Federal Reserve Act *permitted,* but the

3

abnormal world credit situation created by the war *impelled* the striking expansion in American foreign banking facilities after 1914.

An important market for American bank acceptances has been created and they are now used for financing a large part of our foreign trade. The 26 American branch banks in the foreign field before 1914 sprang in less than six years into a system of some 180 branches scattered all over the world. Although after the cessation of the abnormal world trade in 1920 a great many branches were withdrawn, today the system is four times as large as in 1913—and it is again expanding.

The growth of American foreign banking facilities in the decade which opened in 1914 was unprecedented. This book has to do with that interesting and remarkable expansion.

Banks and Branches

Meaning of Foreign Expansion.—What is meant by foreign expansion on the part of banking institutions? For the purpose of this study a bank's foreign expansion is represented by its ownership of banking establishments located without the boundaries of the country in which the bank is domiciled. Banks may undertake foreign expansion by opening branches, by establishing subsidiaries, or by buying into native banks in foreign lands. Some banks have established foreign representatives' offices but these offices do not constitute foreign expansion in its full sense for they only "represent" their home banks and do not engage in regular banking operations in the foreign countries. The foreign expansion of American banks has been almost entirely accomplished through the establishment of foreign branch banks by incorporated commercial banking institutions.

The Branch Bank.—At the outset it is important clearly to understand what is meant by the phrase "foreign branches

of American incorporated commercial banking institutions."
A branch bank is an establishment empowered to carry on the
regular[1] banking operations engaged in by the parent concern,
having no capital really its own, and geographically separated
from the home institution which owns and controls it. A
bank is an institution which specializes in two fundamental
operations.[2] It lends credit to people who have need of it,
or in other words it guarantees the credit of individuals by
substituting therefor the credit of the bank which is acceptable
to everyone. In order to furnish this credit to those in need
of it, the bank borrows from those who have funds to lend.
These two main functions of borrowing and lending credit
are the special characteristics of banking institutions.

Commercial Banks and Their Activity Abroad.—Banking
institutions may be classified in three ways. According to
type of business, banks are either commercial or investment
institutions. According to the legal authority under which
these banks conduct their business, they are either national,
state, or private institutions. With reference to their form of
organization, they are either incorporated or private enterprises.

The main type of business of a commercial bank is the
lending of short-term credits to industry and commerce for
the production and exchange of goods. The business of a
commercial bank is of course not limited solely to the extension
of credit at short term; it engages in a great variety of other
operations, some of which may consist in offering to its clients
safety deposit, fiduciary, and travel agency services, and departments for savings and for the purchase and sale of securities.

In a way it may be said that the average commercial bank
extends a great deal of long-time credit. That is, it invests
heavily in "securities," although not so heavily, ordinarily,
as in bills and notes. The commercial bank borrows most of

---

[1] Branches of national banks may not issue bank notes.
[2] Banks have another function, not generally mentioned, i.e., "clearing." See
R. T. Ely, Outlines of Economics, 4th ed., p. 262.

its money and credit at short term and must lend this money and credit in the same way. Hence, when the more important operations of an establishment are those of extending short-term credits for production and trade we give it the designation of commercial bank or ordinary bank.

American commercial banks may be private enterprises (usually partnerships) or they may be incorporated under the laws of the United States or a state thereof. We are concerned in this study with the American incorporated commercial banking institutions and their foreign branches. The American incorporated commercial banking enterprises which have established or acquired foreign branches and have accounted for practically all of the American foreign banking expansion include national banks, state trust companies,[3] and foreign banking corporations incorporated under state laws. The national banks were: The Chase National Bank of the City of New York, the Commercial National Bank of Washington, D. C., the First National Bank of Boston, and the National City Bank of New York. The state trust companies were: the Bankers Trust Company, the Empire Trust Company, the Equitable Trust Company, the Farmers' Loan and Trust Company, the Guaranty Trust Company, the Jarvis-Conklin Mortgage Trust Company, and the North American Trust Company (name changed in 1905 to Trust Company of America)—all of New York City. The foreign banking corporations included the American Foreign Banking Corporation, the Asia Banking Corporation, the Bank of Central and South America, the Continental Banking and Trust Company of Panama, the Equitable Eastern Banking Corporation, the International Banking Corporation, the Mercantile Bank of

---

[3] The state trust companies mentioned as well as many other American trust companies are to be included in the category of commercial banking institutions as far as type of business is concerned. Some trust companies confine themselves strictly to the business of a trust company. Only one of this class, however, has engaged in foreign expansion. This is the Southern Trust Company of Nogales, Arizona, which was established on January 1, 1922 and has had one branch at Navojoa, Mexico, since May 1, 1925.

the Americas, and the Park-Union Foreign Banking Corporation.

The American incorporated commercial banking institutions which at present have foreign branches are: the national banks with the exception of the Commercial National Bank, the state trust companies with the exception of the last two named, and the Equitable Eastern Banking Corporation and the International Banking Corporation. The private commercial banks located in the United States have not established foreign branches.

Investment Banks in the Foreign Field.—The more important operations of the investment bank consist of borrowing and lending credit at long term. This type of banking institution finances enterprises, floats security issues, and may engage to some extent in commercial banking operations. The investment bank may be either an incorporated institution or a private enterprise organized as a partnership. An example of the incorporated type is the General Motors Acceptance Corporation. This concern has several foreign branches but it operates principally in long-term credits for the special purpose of financing sales on time of General Motors products. The incorporated investment banks doing a general investment banking business have not established branches.

The private investment house interested in foreign banking is represented by a number of well-known American establishments. The American private investment houses have not been inclined to establish foreign branches. Harris, Forbes and Company, New York, it is true, established a branch in London in 1913. The firm confines itself to the handling of high grade investment securities. It does not act as a broker but buys all securities for its own account after careful investigation and offers them to the public. The London office is distinctly a branch of the New York house; it is not organized as a separate establishment nor has it separate capital of its own. Other American private investment houses have not employed the branch method for foreign expansion. The commandite method whereby a bank secures a controlling interest in a foreign native bank and endeavors to manage it to a greater or lesser extent has not found favor with American private houses.

Most of the American private banking institutions which have interests in establishments located abroad have employed the affiliate method. These institutions and their houses (affiliates) abroad are separately organized under the laws of the different countries and are separately managed. The establishment abroad may be entirely owned by some of the partners of the American house, as in the cases of Pynchon and Company and its London house, and J. P. Morgan and Company and its French affiliate, Morgan Harjes and Company of Paris. Often, however, some of the partners of the concern abroad are foreigners. This is true of the affiliates in London of Lee, Higginson and Company, and J. P. Morgan and Company, and also of the Paris office of Munroe and Company. Finally, it is to be remarked that a number of houses abroad bearing similar names to American institutions and commonly spoken of as affiliates of these institutions are completely owned and managed by foreigners. The well-known American houses of Brown Brothers and Company, and J. and W. Seligman and Company have no interests in the London firms of Brown, Shipley and Company, and Seligman Brothers. The New York house of Lazard Frères is the only one of the numerous Lazard houses in which a controlling interest is owned by Americans.

American Private Banking Houses and Their Foreign Connections.—Here brief mention may be made of the several important American private banking houses and their foreign connections. The present partnership of J. P. Morgan and

Company, New York, was constituted in 1895, its predecessor firms having been: J. P. Morgan and Company, 1860 to 1864; Dabney Morgan and Company, 1864 to 1871; Drexel Morgan and Company, 1871 to 1895. The existing Morgan Grenfell and Company partnership, London, was formed in 1910, and the predecessor firm was J. S. Morgan and Company which was founded about 1864. Morgan Harjes and Company, Paris, was organized in 1895, and the prior partnership was Drexel Harjes and Company which was constituted in 1871. The partners of the New York and Paris firms are all American while those of the London house are American and British. These houses are not commercial banks but are "merchants in securities and carry on a private business in banking and exchange."

Pynchon and Company, New York, established an office in London about twenty years ago and later opened another in Liverpool. The firm's business is that of a broker in securities and commodities dealt in on the principal exchanges of this country and it also carries on an investment business. The resident partners of the London house are American citizens and are general members of the firm of Pynchon and Company of which all members are Americans.

The partnerships of Brown Brothers and Company, New York, and Brown, Shipley and Company, London, were established in 1825 and 1863 respectively. Originally the partners in each firm were partners in the other, but during the World War many legal complications arose because of this joint partnership and it was dissolved as of January 1, 1918. Each firm since that date has been separate and distinct and none of the partners in one firm is a member of the other. All the members of the New York partnership are American born.

The firm of J. and W. Seligman and Company, New York, was first established in 1848 to engage in the clothing and importing business. In 1862 the partnership entered the banking business and at that time the London house of Seligman

Brothers was established. The New York firm is composed entirely of American citizens while the London partnership includes only British subjects. Neither firm owns any interests in the other.

Munroe and Company, Paris, was founded in 1851 by an American, John Munroe, who had previously been engaged in the mercantile business in that city. In 1854 the New York partnership of John Munroe and Co., was constituted as a branch office. Almost continuously throughout the existence of the firms, or rather firm, there have been both French and American partners. At present there are three Americans and three Frenchmen; neither group holds a controlling interest.

Lee, Higginson and Company, Boston, was organized in 1848 under the name of Lee and Higginson and changed to the present style in 1853. The London house of Higginson and Company was founded in 1906 under the name of Higginson, Tottie and Company and was changed to Higginson and Company in 1907. All the partners of the Boston house are Americans and resident in the United States except one Englishman who lives abroad. The London firm has its own capital and is managed entirely by three English and two American partners all of whom are resident in London.

The American firm of Lazard Frères was established as a mercantile concern in New Orleans, San Francisco, and New York in 1849. In 1876 the New York house was converted into a private banking firm. The Paris office which was founded in 1849 was likewise turned into a bank in 1876 under the name Lazard Frères & Compagnie. The London House of Lazard Brothers and Company, Ltd., was established in 1877 and it, in turn, opened the Antwerp office in 1918 and the Madrid office in 1920. After the World War the Antwerp office opened a branch at Brussels and the Paris house installed a branch at Mayence. In the New York firm the controlling interest is owned by Americans.

The important American private banking houses, it is clear, have made no appreciable foreign expansion as represented by ownership in banking establishments abroad.

Cuban Agencies of Federal Reserve Banks.—The federal reserve banks represent a class apart from the two general categories of commercial and investment banking institutions. They are bankers' banks, banking institutions instead of the general public constituting their customers. There are at present two agencies in Cuba of federal reserve banks but elsewhere outside the territory of the United States no offices have been established.

Merchants and Travel Agencies.—Before leaving this subject of banks and branches it is interesting to note two kinds of American institutions which have foreign branches and carry on some banking operations but are not banks. The first type is represented by W. R. Grace and Company, New York, and its foreign branches. This company is a merchandising house, organized some three-quarters of a century ago to conduct a general trading business between the Americas. Branches were established throughout South America and in the Orient. As the business of the company developed it naturally followed that a certain amount of banking business was practically thrust upon the home institution and branches. But although the company and its branches fulfill a certain number of banking functions the enterprise cannot be designated as a bank. The second kind of establishment is the regular American travel agency with its branches abroad. Some banking operations are transacted by these concerns but they are not to be classed as banks.[4]

The Branch Method.—Since the establishment of the first American foreign branch bank in 1887 by the Jarvis-Conklin

---

[4] See, however, the American Express Company, Inc., pp. 160–161.

Mortgage Trust Company, New York, the foreign expansion of American banks has been almost entirely accomplished by the establishment of branch banks abroad. The methods of creating subsidiaries or affiliates in foreign countries and buying into native banks abroad have been used only in a very few cases. This foreign expansion by the use of branch banks has not been on the part of private banking houses; it has been made by American incorporated commercial banking institutions: national banks, state trust companies, and state foreign banking corporations. Thus, the study of these banking institutions, with some mention of the foreign branches of the federal reserve banks and of the development of American bank acceptances, will occupy our attention.

The Nationality of Corporations

Necessity for Discussing Nationality.—The necessity of discussing the nationality of banks is not evident unless one understands that a banking institution incorporated in the United States under American laws is not necessarily an "American" corporation in the eyes of the courts of the foreign countries where its branches are located. This is of great practical importance to a bank as well as of academic interest because a bank and its branches have different rights and obligations in a foreign country depending upon the nationality assigned to the bank by the courts of that country.

What determines the nationality of a corporation? The legal experts and the courts of the various nations differ in their answers to this question, and we find four different criteria of nationality employed in distinguishing native corporations from foreign corporations.

The American Criterion.—The courts of the United States hold that a corporation being an artificial creature of the law can have no other nationality than that conferred upon it by the laws of the country (or state) wherein it is organized. Thus in America we give a corporation the nationality of the country in which it was constituted, and pay no attention to the nationality of the people who own it or to the nationality of the country in which its real home office is located. According to the criterion adopted by our courts a bank incorporated under the laws of Italy by five Spaniards would be an Italian corporation; it would be Italian even if its real home office were located at Madrid and all its business done outside of Italy.

No foreign country has adopted this criterion of nationality for continual frauds can be perpetrated under it. In the United States, where it is accepted by the courts, corporations have often taken out their charters under the laws of the states offering the most advantages and the least obligations, thus evading the stricter laws of the states where they wished to operate. New Jersey was for long a Mecca for such corporations, and Delaware, West Virginia, and other states are especially hospitable to them. Foreign nations do not permit this of course. Spain will not allow a foreign corporation chartered as Spanish to escape the obligations of a foreign society. France will not permit a French corporation organized under the laws of England to operate in France as an English corporation.[5] Many other examples might be given.

Thus, the sole fact that a banking corporation has been organized in this country under American laws may mean that it is American for the courts of the United States, but it does not signify that it is of American nationality for the courts of the foreign countries where its branches are located. The foreign court always decides for itself, according to its

---

[5] Rochette et autres. Trib. Corr. de la Seine, July 27, 1910. See Clunet *Journal du Droit International Privé*, 1911, p. 234. The court held that the company was really French, that it was really managed from Paris where its principal establishment was located although its by-laws gave London as its principal place of business, and that it was organized under English laws solely to enable its founders to evade the French law regulating the organization of stock companies, the verification and approval of contributions in kind, the issue and negotiation of shares, etc.

own special criterion, upon the nationality it shall assign to a bank, and the bank is taxed, called upon to fulfill certain formalities, and has rights and obligations according to the nationality assigned to it.

The Center of Exploitation Theory.—Some foreign legal students claim that the nationality of a corporation is that of the country where its principal business interests are located. This is called the theory of the "center of exploitation." Thus a corporation formed by Frenchmen under the laws of the Republic of France and having its home office at Paris but possessing a branch office in Belgium which does more business than the home office would be a Belgian corporation.

This theory has serious drawbacks. Banks and other corporations may have establishments in many countries as they do have today. How is one to determine the center of exploitation? And if one can adjudge this center by comparing the relative amount of business done by the various establishments in a certain year, the following year may find the center of exploitation in another country due to the variations in business which may make the establishment in that country more remunerative. The nationality of a corporation might, thus, be continually subject to change.

The theory of the center of exploitation as a criterion of the nationality of corporations is advocated by a few foreign students but it has not been accepted by the courts. From the law it would seem that this criterion might be applied to corporations for the purpose of determining their nationality by the courts of Belgium (according to Article 129 of the Law of 1873), and by the courts of Italy (Article 230 of the Commercial Code of 1882). However, as stated above, foreign courts have not adopted this theory.

The Home Office as Criterion.—A third criterion determines the nationality of a corporation to be that of the country where its administrative offices, which manage and direct the affairs of the concern, are located. This system is called that of the "siège social" by which is meant the administrative center of the business. To determine the center of administration the courts consider a number of things: the domicile as stated in the constitution and by-laws of the concern, the location of its managing offices, the place or places where the stockholders hold their general meetings, where the books are kept and the inventories made—in short, the courts endeavor to discover neither the place where the corporation is said to be domiciled nor the place where its greatest business is done, but the place from which the operations of the concern are in reality directed.

Up to the war this criterion was applied by most foreign courts, and it still remains the chief system employed outside of the United States. It would seem that this is a better criterion than the first two examined, and that under it a corporation's nationality is not subject to continual change. Yet there is an element of weakness in it. According to this system a group of Germans may create a bank, locate its home office or center of administration at Paris, establish branches throughout France and abroad, and the bank and its branches will be considered to be of French nationality. But suppose a war occurs between France and Germany,— shall this bank and its branches be permitted to go on functioning in the interests of the German capitalists under the false claim that it is a French corporation?

This criterion of nationality, therefore, also permits frauds. Corporations under such a system can masquerade under a nationality other than that of their founders and owners. The seat of administration of a concern may be chosen deliberately with the intention of escaping the provisions of the laws of countries in which it wishes to operate. This leads us to the consideration of a fourth criterion of nationality,—a criterion given great prominence by the World War.

Control as a Criterion.—A final theory, called that of "control," assigns a corporation the nationality of the people who control the dominating interests in it. In determining the nationality of a concern the courts inquire into the nationality of the persons who own a controlling portion of the capital and of those who manage the enterprise. Sometimes even the object of the corporation has determined its nationality to the satisfaction of the court; the Court of Algiers held that a company having its administrative or home office at Rotterdam, Holland, but which had for its object the sale of German products was of German nationality.[6]

The European courts did not employ this criterion before the war because it permits the nationality of a corporation to change due to the cession of stocks by persons of one nationality to those of another. However, during the war it had to be adopted by the European nations and by others as well in the interests of national defense. There were corporations owned and directed by German capitalists but having some other nationality, according to the criteria of nationality then employed, which were operating in the allied and associated nations and vice versa.

The courts of all countries having in their territory corporations controlled by subjects of enemy nations adopted the criterion of "control" in determining the nationality of such concerns, and placed them in the hands of a public custodian of enemy alien property. It should be observed, however, that the criterion of "control" has been applied to determine the nationality of corporations only in the case of those establishments controlled by enemy interests,—although there is nothing to prohibit its application to other enterprises.[7]

This criterion of nationality was not employed by European courts before the war, as just mentioned, except in Spain

---

[6] Cour d'Alger, July 22, 1915; Clunet, *rev. cit.*, 1915, p. 903.
[7] P. Barazzetti as a good treatment of the system of "control" in his Régime des Banques Etrangères dans les Principales Législations, pp. 12–19. See also E. H. Young, Foreign Companies, on the nationality of corporations.

where the courts were permitted by Article 4 of the Royal
Decree of April 25, 1911 to assign a foreign nationality to a
corporation located in Spain for *taxation* purposes: (1) if
the administrative officers are of foreign nationality; (2) if
they are employed by a foreign establishment; (3) if it appears
that the concern in Spain is dependent upon a foreign organization; or (4) if a controlling part of the capital of the
corporation in question is possessed by foreigners.

A Hypothetical Case.—From the examination of these
different criteria it is evident that several nationalities might
conceivably be assigned to one bank according to the criteria
employed by the courts of the countries where its branches
are located. Suppose several Americans incorporate a bank
under the laws of Italy and establish branches at New York,
Paris, Brussels, and Madrid. They live in Spain directing
the business from Madrid and after some time it happens that
the branch at Paris does the most business year after year.
What would be the nationality of the bank and its branches?
It would be Italian for the American courts because the bank
was incorporated under the laws of Italy; Spanish for the
French courts since its administrative office is at Madrid;
American, at least for the purpose of taxation, according to
Spanish law for the capital and control of the bank is possessed
by Americans; and finally, the bank might be called French by
some foreign writers for its center of exploitation is at Paris.

In face of this diversity between the criteria of nationality
of corporations it is to be hoped that the financial and economic
commission of the League of Nations or the International
Chamber of Commerce may take steps to bring the laws of
the various nations into agreement upon a criterion of nationality.

When is a Bank "American"?—Which criterion of nationality is to be accepted in this study? Since we are consider-

ing the expansion outside the boundaries of the United States by incorporated commercial banking institutions located within this country, it naturally follows that these institutions are of American nationality under the "country of incorporation" and the "home office" criteria. But the mere fact that a commercial banking institution has been incorporated under American laws and has its home office in the United States does not make it "American" for the purposes of this study. It must be in reality American, i.e., it must be owned and controlled by American capital. There are a number of banking establishments which are incorporated under American laws and which have home offices in the United States but are owned or controlled by foreign capital (see p. 201). However, it appears that only one of these has engaged in foreign expansion—the Sonora Bank and Trust Company. This bank was incorporated under the laws of the State of Arizona on May 25, 1914, and has its head office at Nogales, Arizona, but is controlled by Mexican citizens. It has four branches in Mexico which are located at Culiacan, Guaymas, Hermosillo and Navojoa.

An examination of the incorporated commercial banking institutions which have expanded abroad from the United States will show that all are recognized as American either under the "country of incorporation" criterion or the "home office" criterion or the criterion of "control" (with the exception of the one bank mentioned above). These three criteria are those which are in general use and so it is evident that there can be little dispute as to which banks are to be included in a study of the foreign expansion of American banks. Only the advocates of the theory of the "center of exploitation" might criticize. They would have to grant American nationality under their theory to the banks and trust companies domiciled in the United States which have expanded abroad, but they might possibly assign other nationalities than American to some of the American foreign banking corporations—small corporations owned and controlled by American capital, organized under American laws, and directed from home offices in the United States but whose operations in some foreign country may be larger than those at the head offices in this country. This theory has but very small acceptance, is not applied by the courts, and need not detain us here.

Having considered in the preceding pages the meaning of foreign expansion, the nature of banking institutions, and the criteria of nationality, we may state the main object of the present study to be an examination of the establishment and acquisition of banking concerns outside the boundaries of the United States by incorporated commercial banking institutions organized under American laws, domiciled in the United States, and owned and controlled by American capital.

CHAPTER II

METHODS OF BANKING CONTACT WITH FOREIGN MARKETS

The Connection between Foreign Trade and Foreign Banking.—The expansion of commercial bank branches in foreign markets since the middle of the nineteenth century shows clearly the close connection which exists between the growth of foreign trade and the development of overseas banking organizations. While, on the one hand, commerce necessitates for its expansion a growing and efficient system of commercial banks, on the other hand, the banks exist and prosper only because they facilitate commercial operations. Hence, when one considers the export of capital and the great foreign trade of England before the war, it is not surprising that the great British foreign and colonial banks had so large a system of branches in the countries with which they conducted such a volume of commercial transactions.

At the beginning of the decade preceding the war, England had 32 colonial banks with head offices in London, and 2,104 branches in the colonies besides 18 other British foreign banks with 175 branches. At this same time France had 18 colonial banks with 104 offices; Germany, 13 with about 70 branches, and Holland, 16 oversea banks with 68 branches. The branches that the banks of the above countries possessed in certain foreign markets owed their existence to European export of capital and to the volume of trade between the European nations and these foreign markets. Reciprocally, the systems of branch banks tended to have some effect toward increasing the volume of foreign trade.

Methods of Foreign Banking Contact.—Now a commercial bank may employ a number of arrangements for its operations with foreign markets, depending upon the importance of the business transacted with any one country or center, upon foreign and domestic banking legislation, and also upon special considerations affecting the policy of the particular bank.

In those markets with which the bank's operations are small, the bank will transact its business through a native bank or through the branch of a foreign bank acting as correspondent. In others with which the operations of the bank are sizeable, the bank will employ additional methods in order to secure a better connection than that offered by the correspondent. Some banks follow a policy of co-operating with foreign establishments—for example the American Exchange Irving Trust Company and the National Bank of Commerce—and install representatives in their chief foreign markets to obtain better correspondent relations through close co-operation. Other banks undertake actual expansion into the countries with which they have, or expect to have, a large volume of business.

The Correspondent

The General Use of the Correspondent Method.—The most general method of transacting banking operations with a foreign market is by employing the services of a native bank or of a branch of a foreign bank in that market to act as correspondent. Every great bank has a list of thousands of banks abroad with which it has established correspondent relations. This simply means that the bank has made arrangements with these foreign banks whereby it agrees to act as agent for them and they as agents for it. It is due to this arrangement, for example, that letters of credit issued by a home bank can be cashed by tourists at correspondents of that bank in nearly every city in the world. When a New York bank has business to do in a foreign market it transacts it through its correspondent at that place, dividing the commission, and when the correspondent has business to transact in the United States it sends it through the New York bank.

A bank which is in constant relation with a correspondent, drawing bills on it and accepting bills drawn by the correspondent, collecting for it, etc., usually keeps an account or balance at the correspondent bank. In the majority of cases, however, the business transacted by a bank with its correspondent is not of such a continuous nature, and when a bank does a steady and fair-sized volume of business with a foreign center it usually begins to think of establishing a branch of its own there or of securing a better banking contract by other means. It may cease to co-operate with its correspondent and begin to compete with it.

Reasons for the General Use of the Correspondent Method.—The great use by American banks of the correspondent method in dealing with foreign markets is due fundamentally to the multiplicity of relatively small banks under our independent banking system, most of these banks carrying on only small and intermittent operations with given foreign centers. The amount of business done by any one of such banks is insufficient to support a branch bank or even a foreign representative's office.

Some of the large New York banks prefer the correspondent system to branches. The explanation of this attitude is due in part to the fact that many of even these great institutions do not carry on a large enough volume of business with any one foreign center to warrant the establishment of a branch bank. These banks which favor the correspondent system as opposed to all others also argue that old established foreign institutions with their great experience, their intimate knowledge of their own country, and their large nets of domestic branches are able to offer a superior service in furnishing information on local credit conditions, handling documents, and making collections. The enthusiastic supporters of the correspondent method, in short, can see no necessity for foreign banking expansion.

The International Acceptance Bank, Inc., New York City, in which a number of foreign banks hold stock, has made it a part of institutional policy to conduct all its foreign operations by correspondents. H. J. Rogers, assistant vice-president of the bank, writes, "We have never opened branches of any sort either in this country or abroad, as we have made it a policy to co-operate with stockholding banks and banking houses in the important countries abroad where we extend credit. In this way we obtain more expert advice on the various financial propositions that arise than would be possible on a competitive basis." The bank was established in April, 1921 and has enjoyed a good measure of success which F. A. Goodhue, its president, states "may be attributed in a great measure to the valuable co-operation of its intimate friends abroad."

Fear of Risks in Foreign Branch Banking.—Most banks do not, as the International Acceptance Bank, have stockholding institutions among their correspondents, but, nevertheless, prefer the correspondent system. They fear the risks attending the establishment of branches in foreign countries, and they further argue that the establishment of a branch bank in a foreign market will cause the parent bank to lose valuable business originating from that market through its correspondents there. The correspondents of the bank will naturally not wish to retain as their agent in the United States a bank which is competing with them in their own territory; they will prefer a non-competing American bank. There is much truth in this argument; not only will the bank installing a branch lose some correspondent business, but, in addition, the branch will do well to make expenses at the outset if it does not prove a definite loss during the first few years.[1]

The Representative

Employed to Supplement Correspondents.—Banks which have built up an appreciable business, or which hope to increase their business, with certain foreign centers employ other methods of foreign banking contact in addition to their foreign correspondents. One of these methods is that of locating a representative's office in a foreign city. Such foreign representatives' offices differ from a branch bank in that they do not receive deposits nor engage in the regular banking operations which bring a branch into active competition with the native banks. They act rather as "service stations" as stated in the letter quoted (p. 25), sending information to the home office, aiding American commercial travelers and tourists abroad, and bringing the home bank's correspondents in foreign cities into closer relations with it.

The essence of the relation between a bank and its correspondents is co-operation and the establishment of foreign representatives' offices is the logical outgrowth of a policy which seeks to secure better relations with foreign markets without entering into competition with the bank's correspondents in those markets. The establishment of foreign branch banks or subsidiaries or the securing of a controlling interest in native banks in a foreign center means the abandonment of a policy of co-operation with the bank's correspondents in that center for one of competition. It means the actual expansion of the bank into the territory of its correspondent.

---

[1] Cf. *Journal of Commerce*, October 21, 1919, "As for the branch question itself, a good many American banks have been of the opinion that it was not wise for them to attempt to compete abroad with locally organized foreign institutions. Some have advertised that they preferred to 'work with foreign banks in the friendly countries.' The scramble for trade since the armistice has tended to convince a good many bankers that this idea was erroneous and that the foreign bankers were usually not willing to give up trade to them, but merely regarded their correspondent relationship as an incident in their business. They found out from the bills passing through their hands where the trade was going and they then endeavored to take it over, in many cases succeeding."

Several Institutions with Foreign Representatives.—The American Exchange Irving Trust Company,[2] New York, was the result of a merger late in 1926 between the Irving Bank and Trust Company and the American Exchange-Pacific National Bank. The Irving Bank–Columbia Trust Company (after September 20, 1926 the Irving Bank and Trust Company) adopted in 1916 the foreign representative method as a means of securing better correspondent relationships and established foreign representatives' offices at London, Paris, Berlin, Mexico City and Bombay. Concerning these offices, G. A. O'Reilly, former vice-president of the Irving Bank–Columbia Trust Company, writes:

These offices are service stations rather than branches. They keep us informed upon foreign exchange activities in important centers and upon credit, financial and commercial conditions in fields in which we operate. They also serve as centers of assistance and information for our customers traveling abroad or interested in particular countries.

In our plan of organization and operation, these offices meet the banks of the countries in which they are established upon a basis of co-operation rather than of competition. They do not take deposits or conduct a banking business. Through them we have been able to secure from foreign correspondent banks a measure of co-operation which would be exceedingly difficult, if not entirely impossible, under a competitive plan. In this way correspondent relations, ordinarily most perfunctory, frequently develop into something very well worth while.

The National Bank of Commerce in New York[3] is another great American bank which has established foreign representatives' offices to render its correspondent relationships more satisfactory. The bank established offices in London and Copenhagen in 1919 and installed a third at Paris in 1925.

---

[2] The merger was approved by the directors of both institutions on October 14, 1926. Condition of the American Exchange Irving Trust Company in December, 1926: capital $32,000,000; surplus and undivided profits $26,000,000; deposits $677,000,000; total resources $735,000,000. The condition of the Irving Bank–Columbia Trust Company on June 30, 1926 was: capital $17,500,000; surplus and undivided profits $14,444,131; deposits $345,475,888; total resources $446,228,799.

[3] Statement of condition on June 30, 1926: capital $25,000,000; surplus $35,000,000; undivided profits $6,942,978; deposits $515,005,640; total resources $631,401,666.

With reference to these offices, R. R. McElvare, manager of the Service Department of the bank, writes:

Aside from those functions which might be performed by a correspondent bank, our representatives act as liaison officers with our correspondents and thus promote closer working relationships.

In foreign relations the National Bank of Commerce in New York has pursued the policy which it has followed in its domestic business. Through years of co-operative effort and activity, it has built up close correspondent relations with the strongest banks throughout the world. In many cases these correspondents include the governmental institutions of their respective countries. Thus its customers are afforded the facilities of the best native connections wherever they seek business, with an intimate knowledge of local conditions which it is so difficult for any foreign competitive bank to acquire.

To facilitate relations with our correspondents abroad, co-operate with our customers in foreign transactions, and gather information on commercial, economic and other conditions in Europe, offices of resident representatives were established in London, Copenhagen, and Paris.

Through travel and personal contacts our representatives and officers keep in close touch with all of our correspondents and with affairs abroad. We find the use of resident and traveling representatives suitable to our needs and favor this system rather than the establishment of direct foreign branches.

The advantages of systems of foreign representatives' offices are well put in the two letters quoted. The combination of foreign representatives' offices with carefully chosen foreign correspondent banks raises international banking on the co-operative basis to its highest efficiency.

Before leaving this subject of foreign representatives it is interesting to note the special arrangement made by the Farmers' Loan and Trust Company,[4] New York, in installing its representative at Paris. This institution was the first American bank to establish a branch in France, opening its doors for business in Paris in 1906. It was successful and

---

[4] See pp. 139–141.

was especially helpful during the World War in financing Franco-American trade and in extending banking services to the American expeditionary forces. The National City Bank of New York was desirous of entering the Paris market and finally on December 31, 1921 purchased the Paris branch of the Farmers' Loan and Trust Company, and has been profitably running it ever since. Some agreement was no doubt reached whereby the Farmers' Loan and Trust Company would not open another branch in Paris as this bank has since January 1, 1922 transacted its French business through a representative in Paris.

The representative is attached to a great French bank, the Banque de Paris et des Pays-Bas, where his office is located. The cost of maintenance of the representative's office is very low, and the representative is in the best position to secure excellent correspondent relations through close co-operation. He is received by the personnel of the French bank almost as if he were employed by the bank, the services of which he has at his disposition as if it were his own institution. He is easy of access to the clients of the French bank who may wish to avail themselves of his services and is able to secure business in this way for the parent establishment at New York. By means of this representative the Farmers' Loan and Trust Company has been able to continue to accommodate its American clients stopping in or passing through Paris and to maintain an excellent correspondent relation.

Value of the Foreign Representative.—These methods of installing representatives abroad are attractive to a bank for the expenses are lower than those of a branch, and the services rendered to the bank are of far greater importance than those obtained from a simple correspondent relationship. If the business done by an American bank with a foreign center is large enough or promises to become sufficient to cover in a satisfactory manner the expenses of a representative's office the bank has every reason to proceed to the establishment of one for, as previously stated, the combination of a representative with the bank's correspondents in a foreign market is far superior to the method of dealing solely by correspondents.

The Commandite

Actual Foreign Banking Expansion.—But few banks are satisfied to transact their business with a foreign center through correspondents or correspondents and representatives when their business with that center is large or promises to become large. Under such conditions banks are led to make expansion into the foreign market by the acquisition or creation of regular banking establishments. The commandite is one method of foreign expansion. The commandite method consists in buying an interest, usually a controlling interest, in a native bank in that foreign market with which a bank wishes to improve its relations.[5] The native institution in which the bank secures control is called a commandite and the process is called commanditing. The commandited native bank may retain its external appearances and its good will but it is directed to a greater or lesser degree by the bank which has gained control of it.

German Banks and Commandites.—This was the method employed very often by the great German banks in their foreign expansion before the war, and indeed was the very first method used by them. As early as 1854 the Darmstädter bank founded a commandite in the United States, buying an interest in the G. Vom Baur and Company, New York City. The great Deutsche Bank which was the leader in German foreign expansion entered the field in 1872 by commanditing

---

[5] The word affiliate is also used to denote a bank in which another bank has an interest. The commandite method differs from the affiliate method in that its object is not only to obtain an interest in a separate institution but also to control and direct it as much as possible. The affiliate method has been used by American private investment houses in foreign expansion but it does not appear to have been used by American incorporated commercial banks.

Knoblauch & Lichtenstein, New York, and establishing two branches at Yokohama and Shanghai. The branches were in difficulties from the start and were closed in 1874 but the commandite was not liquidated until October 15, 1882. The Deutsche Bank commandited other foreign banks: Weissweiller and Goldschmidt at Paris in 1873, Güterbock, Horwitz and Company at Vienna in 1877, Rosenfeld and Company at Vienna in 1895, and Guillermo Vogel and Company at Madrid in 1895.

The policy of commanditing foreign banks was very generally followed by all the great German banks because it represented an easy method of access to the foreign fields and usually a relatively inexpensive one.[6] A new bank, and above all a foreign bank, has more or less trouble, in conditions of normal credit, in thrusting itself into a market already served by established banks. The new or foreign bank must create good will and find business in a territory already adjusted to the services of existing banking institutions. It may very often fail to secure a foothold, especially if it be a foreign bank; in many instances this has been the case. On the other hand it is evident that the method of commanditing or buying control in an established bank is a sure and certain way of entering a market even if economic conditions are such that not one extra bank could be supported for the time being by the state of the market. The native bank is established and earning its way, and nothing happens but the silent changing of control,—not even the bank's name changes. The only difficulty is in securing the control of the desired bank. This varies, of course, depending upon particular circumstances. The Germans were very successful in thus acquiring control of native banks in foreign countries in their expansion before the World War. In many cases they were able to control a foreign bank by obtaining possession of only a very small

---

[6] The commandite method may also be used to enter a foreign country which prohibits the establishment of branch banks or which taxes the entire capital of a bank installing branches. See pp. 34–35.

amount of the stock, and so they were able to have controlled concerns abroad at an outlay well below that which the creation of branch banks would have entailed.

Advantages and Disadvantages of the Commandite Method.—The commandite method possesses another advantage than that of easy entrance to a foreign market at moderate expense. The controlling bank is not directly liable for its commandited banks as is the parent bank for its branches. The commandite has a capital entirely separate from that of the leading bank and thus the risk of foreign operations is limited to the amount invested in securing the control of the commandite.

But if the commandite be sometimes easier and cheaper than the branch method for gaining an entrance into a foreign field, it is also true that the commandite is more difficult to control than a branch, and the more successful it becomes the greater are the difficulties of the leading bank in trying to control and direct it. Many times it is very difficult to change the accounting methods of the commandited bank, and where it is administered by a local board of directors much interference may develop on the part of native interests. The controlling bank cannot interfere if the manager of the commandite is unsatisfactory as it can in the case of a branch. Thus the connection between the leading bank and its commandite is much looser than that between the parent bank and its branch. It should also be noted that often some of the commandited bank's local business will be lost when it is learned that foreign interests have secured its control.

As a means of obtaining easy access to a market on a paying basis from the very start the commandite may be superior in some cases to a branch which may experience difficulties in forcing itself into a foreign center and must wait some time before it has built up a paying business. But once established, the branch is without question superior to the commandite for administrative purposes because it obeys the direction of the parent bank and works exclusively for the common interest, while commandites have often given their controlling banks much trouble and in some cases have developed contrary banking policies.

The Present Use of the Commandite Method.—American incorporated commercial banking institutions have not looked with favor upon the commandite method. From 1922 until 1925 the Banque Nationale de la République d'Haiti stood in the relation of commandite to the National City Bank of New York. In 1925 the Banque became a subsidiary of the American bank, the bank acquiring the entire capital stock of the institution. Another New York bank experimented with the policy of securing interests in banks in the Orient but shortly adopted the branch bank method of expansion. A war-time American foreign banking corporation (pp. 154–6) made some use of the commandite method and found that the joint American and foreign management of the commandited banks was not without appreciable disadvantages. The commandite method has had but little application by banks other than those of Germany,[7] and its unsatisfactory features have led these establishments to look upon it with ever lessening favor during the last two decades. As Riesser says, ... "It is only natural . . . . that the establishment and maintenance of commandites tends to become rare in the German banking world."[8]

The Subsidiary

Domestic and Foreign Subsidiary Banks.—The foreign subsidiary bank or the domestic subsidiary corporation with

---

[7] With reference to American foreign banking expansion, L. M. Jay, vice-president of the International Banking Corporation, writes, "I know of no American bank having control, or even partial control, of any foreign bank."

[8] Riesser, "Die Deutschen Grossbanken und ihre Konzentration in Zusammenhang mit der Entwicklung des Gesamtwirtschaft in Deutschland," p. 684.

foreign branches is another method of foreign banking expansion which has been employed by the great banks of the world. A subsidiary bank is an establishment entirely owned and controlled by the parent institution or institutions. Unlike a branch it is a separate corporation.

The Equitable Eastern Banking Corporation created by the Equitable Trust Company, the Park-Union Foreign Banking Corporation founded by the National Park Bank of New York and the Union Bank of Canada, and the American Foreign Banking Corporation formed by a large number of American concerns and a Canadian bank are some examples of foreign banking expansion through the establishment of domestic subsidiary corporations which in turn installed branches abroad.

The National City Bank of New York (France) S. A., in Paris and the Banque Nationale de la République d'Haiti are examples of foreign expansion through the acquisition of subsidiary banks located abroad.

American banks have also created domestic subsidiary corporations to engage solely in foreign banking but to carry on their operations through correspondents as opposed to branches. Of these corporations, the First National Corporation and the Shawmut Corporation of Boston, subsidiaries of the First National and Shawmut banks of Boston, may be mentioned. Their foreign banking business through correspondent banks abroad has fallen off since the early post-war years and their business at present consists chiefly in dealing in United States Government securities, bankers' acceptances, and high grade general investments.

The Subsidiary the Favorite German Method.—In the German foreign banking expansion the subsidiary method was the favorite, and not only were subsidiary banks created in Germany to engage in foreign branch banking but also many subsidiaries were installed abroad which in turn established branches both within and without the territory wherein they were located. The great German banks :[9] the Deutsche Bank, the Disconto-Gesellschaft, the A. Schaaffenhausen'scher Bank-Verein, the Dresdner Bank, the Darmstädter Bank, the Berliner Handels-Gesellschaft, and the National Bank für Deutschland tended to co-operate in creating these subsidiaries rather than proceeding individually. The German subsidiary banks were formed to facilitate trade with specific foreign markets.

Domestic Subsidiaries for Foreign Branch Banking.— Some of these subsidiaries were located in the great ports of Germany, for example, the Brasilianische Bank für Deutschland founded in Hamburg in 1887 for better commercial banking connections with Brazil, the Bank für Chile und Deutschland located at Hamburg in 1895 to develop trade between the two countries, and the Deutsch-Ost-Afrikanische Bank formed at Berlin in 1904–5. These banks established foreign branches in the countries with which they were created to operate.

Foreign Subsidiaries.—In many cases the subsidiary banks were located in the country with which and in which it was desired to foster German business. Examples of these were: the Deutsch-Asiatische Bank founded at Shanghai in 1889 for German trade with the Orient, the Banca Commerciale Italiana for trade with Italy established in 1894 at Milan, the Banca Generala Romana formed at Bucharest in 1897 for German-Roumanian commerce, the Banque Internationale de Bruxelles founded at Brussels in 1898 to facilitate trade with Belgium, and the Banque de Crédit installed at Sophia in 1905 for trade between Bulgaria and Germany. These foreign subsidiaries established branches in the countries where

---

[9] The Disconto-Gesellschaft absorbed the A. Schaaffenhausen'scher Bank-Verein in 1914. The Darmstädter Bank (Bank für Handel und Industrie) and the National Bank für Deutschland merged in 1921, forming the Darmstädter und National Bank.

they operated and sometimes abroad. The Banca Commerciale Italiana established 35 branches in Italy within the first fifteen years of its existence besides several other branches in important foreign centers. The Deutsch-Asiatische Bank at Shanghai founded 12 branches in the Orient within the first decade of operation.

The subsidiary banks were in practically all cases formed by several of the great German banks co-operating. There were few exceptions to this rule, that of the Deutsche Bank being the most notable. This institution created a domestic subsidiary of its own, known as the Deutsche Uberseeische Bank, in 1893 for the purpose of establishing foreign branches. The latter bank had some 25 branches abroad at the beginning of the World War.

Reasons for the Use of the Subsidiary Method.—The chief reason for the establishment of domestic or foreign subsidiary banks for foreign banking operations seems to be the desire upon the part of the interested institution or institutions to minimize the risks of foreign banking. By creating separate and special corporations for foreign banking operations banks seek to avoid such risks in that they do not participate directly in foreign operations; their losses are limited by the amounts invested in the corporations. This point has been mentioned in discussing commandites.

The subsidiary method is of real value to a bank contemplating expansion into a country which forbids the establishment of branches by foreign banks or which taxes the entire capital of banks installing branches. In the first case it is necessary to form a subsidiary under the laws of the country in question or secure an interest in a native bank. In the second case it is to be noted that the American banks interested in foreign operations have very large capital and if their branches must pay taxes not only upon the capital employed in the foreign country but also upon the entire capital of the parent institution such branches are at a distinct disadvantage in competing with the native banks in a foreign country. The foreign branches of the subsidiary of an American bank or the subsidiaries organized under the laws of a foreign country by the bank will have a very much smaller taxable capital and will find themselves upon a more equal footing in competition with native establishments. The branches of the National City Bank of New York at Madrid and Barcelona were transferred to the bank's subsidiary, the International Banking Corporation, in 1920, and the bank's Paris branch was changed into a subsidiary corporation under French laws in 1925 in order to escape taxation by Spain and France of the entire capital of the bank.

Other advantages may be ascribed to the subsidiary method. In China branches of American subsidiary banks have been permitted to issue their notes tax-free whereas state bank note issues are subject to a confiscatory tax of 10 per cent. The International Banking Corporation had $2,874,550 of notes in circulation in China on June 30, 1926. Subsidiary corporations formed under state laws to engage only in foreign banking enjoy greater powers than the banking institutions incorporated under federal or state law to carry on both a domestic and foreign business. The charter of the International Banking Corporation, for example, after enumerating its powers for foreign operations granted it the right "to engage in any other lawful business whatsoever."

Position of Large and Small Banks.—The choice between a policy of establishing direct foreign branches and that of creating a foreign subsidiary or a domestic subsidiary to extend branches abroad can, of course, only present itself to the great bank. Here the bank must compare the actual advantages of the two systems in the particular fields in which expansion is envisaged. The small bank is not strong enough by itself to do more than deal with foreign lands by the cor-

respondent method. It may possibly find it advantageous
to co-operate with other banks in forming a foreign banking
corporation to operate with foreign countries either by correspondents or by both correspondents and branches. The
American Foreign Banking Corporation which was owned by
some 36 banks in 33 different cities of the United States was
an example of such co-operation among many banks in forming a domestic subsidiary for foreign branch banking.

Relationship between Subsidiary and Parent Bank.—In
leaving this topic the relation between the subsidiary and the
parent bank or banks must be noted. The foreign subsidiary
of a great bank may be for all practical purposes the same
thing as a direct branch. The National City Bank's subsidiary
at Paris which was formerly a direct branch of the bank is a
case in point. How closely the foreign subsidiary will re-
semble a branch will depend upon to what extent it is directed
and controlled by the home office. In the case of the domestic
subsidiary and the parent bank, the relation between the bank
and the foreign branches of this subsidiary will naturally be
somewhat less direct than that between the bank and its own
foreign branches. This point may be outweighed by other
considerations presented by the particular problem, for example, desire of the bank to confine the risks of foreign
operations or of operations with certain foreign parts (for
example, with the Orient) to a separate organization, or desire
to enter a foreign country taxing the entire capital of banks
installing branches. However, American banks like to establish direct branches wherever possible in order to secure more
direct administration. The National City Bank of New York
took over the seven branches in San Domingo of its subsidiary,
the International Banking Corporation, and made them its
own direct branches on December 31, 1925 "for administrative
purposes." In April, 1926 the bank took over the two
branches in Panama established over twenty years ago by the

corporation. The bank is now dealing with the Western Hemisphere and with Europe (except in the case of France and Spain for reasons already mentioned) through its own direct branches, and with the Far East through the subsidiary and its foreign branches. The Equitable Trust Company which controls the only other American domestic subsidiary corporation with foreign branches operates upon a similar policy, the company having direct branches in Europe and in Mexico and the Equitable Eastern Banking Corporation possessing branches in the Orient.

American Banks and the Subsidiary Method.—Where the subsidiary is owned by a number of banks its effectiveness may be reduced by the feeling among the owning enterprises that the business of the corporation is being diverted from it to certain members, or that they are not getting out of the corporation as much as they should. Such cases presented themselves in the short American experience with this type of foreign trade bank.[10] At present there are no American foreign banking corporations having branches abroad and owned by a large number of banking and business interests. Six concerns of this type operated during the war and post-war periods and then were liquidated: the American Foreign Banking Corporation, the Asia Banking Corporation, the Bank of Central and South America, the Continental Banking and Trust Company of Panama, the Mercantile Bank of the Americas, and the Park-Union Foreign Banking Corporation. Only two other American foreign banking corporations have been formed; the International Banking Corporation, founded in 1901 and since 1915 the subsidiary of the National City Bank of New York, and the Equitable Eastern Banking Cor-

---

[10] H. P. Willis, Federal Reserve System, p. 1229, "It soon appeared that the bank stockholders in such institutions were inclined to suspect one another, or to fear that through some lack of loyalty one or the other of them would be disadvantaged through the knowledge of its transactions or operations gained by the foreign trade bank in which it took stock and to which it agreed to shift presumably much of its foreign business. This factor, therefore, operated quite as strongly as any other in retarding the success of the proposed system of foreign trade banks . . . . it was fairly clear before the end of the year 1916 that not very much could be expected in that direction."

poration created in 1920 by the Equitable Trust Company.
The first-mentioned corporation is owned by the National
City Bank and the other is controlled by the Equitable Trust
Company. They are in profitable operation.

The Branch

Close Relationship Between Bank and Branch.—When
a bank carries on a large volume of operations with a certain
foreign center or when it is persuaded that its business with
this center can be increased to a figure considered sufficient,
the bank tends to establish a branch at that point due to the
advantages of the branch over other methods of foreign banking contact. These advantages spring mainly from the fact
that the ties which unite a correspondent, commandite, or
foreign subsidiary to the bank are much less solid and direct
than those which connect a foreign branch bank to the home
office.

The legal relation which exists between a bank and its foreign correspondent is that which obtains between a principal
and an agent. Generally speaking, the correspondent bank is
supposed to carry out all usual banking transactions for its
principal in the way that such transactions should be executed,
and it is legally responsible to the bank for which it is acting
in case of loss occasioned by negligence or bad faith.

The moral relation between bank and correspondent permits the bank to demand only that the correspondent act with
average efficiency and use due diligence in the execution of
transactions entrusted to it. In the event of a failure of the
correspondent to meet all the bank's expectations in regard
to the furtherance of its interests, the bank can do nothing
unless the correspondent's action or absence of action results
in a loss due to error or bad faith. In this case the bank
might bring action against its correspondent, but this is a
very slow and unsatisfactory procedure in a foreign land

where customs and laws differ from those in the bank's country, and would naturally result in a cessation of all future relations between the bank and its agent.

Control of the Bank over the Branch.—The control of a bank over a branch is more complete than over a correspondent because the branch, being the property of the parent institution, must obey orders given it by the home office while the correspondent bank does not have to do so. The branch is simply a part of the bank itself, and is in all reality just as closely knitted up to the home institution as if it were in the home office building. From the legal point of view the foreign branch is not a separate institution but an integral part of the parent bank,[11] just as in practical operation the branch may be considered to consist of a few rooms of the bank which are outside the main building, perhaps distant in terms of miles, but as completely under the control of the administration as if located in the building. Hence to deal with the foreign branch is to deal with the bank itself. When one enters the branch of an American bank in Buenos Aires it is as if he were standing in one of the rooms of the home office in New York.

The branch is not only compelled to obey orders but, being a part of the parent organization and partaking of its good or bad fortune, it naturally takes a greater interest in serving its own institution, works with more diligence, and goes to greater lengths in looking after the common interest than does the correspondent. "It is only natural that a branch bank will put itself out more for its own institution than would a correspondent which acts for a number of institutions and perhaps has no special incentive to make any particular effort

---

[11] The attorney general (A.G. 601) held that "the parent bank with its branches is one association . . . . and all transactions are regarded as those of one corporation or institution." The regulations of the Federal Reserve Board declare: No. 25–100, "Branch banks have no separate corporate existence; . . . . the national bank and all its branches should be treated as one corporation"; No. 25–102, "A foreign branch established by a national bank is not an independent corporation and the creditors of the branch are creditors of the parent bank."

for any one of them," writes Lawrence Slade, former sub-manager of the Paris branch of one of the great American banks.

The Use of the Branch Method by American Banks.—
The commandite or affiliate and the subsidiary are separate corporations and legally distinct from the leading bank, and although they may be preferable to the correspondent for the conduct of a large volume of banking operations with a foreign center, they are not as directly related to the bank as are its own branches, and may not function as perfectly in the execution of the bank's policy.   Thus, when the great American banks have felt able to embark upon a policy of foreign expansion, i.e., to make the outlay and run the risk of establishing a connection abroad of the importance of a commandite, subsidiary, or branch, they have chosen the branch method except in cases where special considerations have intervened.

The eight greatest American banks, leaders in foreign and domestic banking operations, are: the National City Bank, the Chase National Bank, The American Exchange Irving Trust Company, the Guaranty Trust Company, the National Bank of Commerce, the First National Bank of Boston, the Equitable Trust Company, and the Bankers Trust Company. Not one of these banks has contented itself with a simple system of foreign correspondents.   The National Bank of Commerce and the American Exchange Irving Trust Company have foreign representatives' offices to better their correspondent relationships.   The other six great banks have undertaken foreign expansion, and have principally employed the branch bank method for this purpose.   Two other American banks which are important but not among the first eight, the Farmers' Loan and Trust Company and the Empire Trust Company, also have foreign branches.

CHAPTER III

BRANCH BANKS AND FOREIGN TRADE FINANCING

Advantages of Foreign Branch Banks.—This and the following chapter are devoted to the explanation of the general reasons for the establishment of foreign branch banks, and examine in some detail the various advantages claimed for the branch method in financing and promoting a nation's foreign trade. The question of the branch bank's advantages is the subject of much controversy. The student of economics approaches the question from a general and broad viewpoint, points out the fact that the advantages of the foreign branch bank are greatly overexaggerated by the writers on trade promotion and by business men, and very often leaves the impression that there is little reason for the establishment of branch banks abroad. The bankers of the world, studying the question from the individual viewpoint of their own business, proceed to establish thousands of foreign branch banks. Both parties are right: a nations foreign trade may get along without the establishment of its own branch banks and the necessity for such branch bank establishment is usually exaggerated; but there are evidently reasons for foreign branch bank establishment and it is true that branch banks do contribute to the promotion of a country's foreign trade. In this study we will consider not so much the old debated question: why is there any necessity for the establishment of foreign branch banks, as the question: why were American foreign branch banks established? What, in effect, were the advantages, real or of doubtful value, that appealed to American bankers?

Perhaps substantial agreement might be reached in the

evaluation of the branch bank if we were to keep constantly
in mind the fact that it is impossible to select some one of the
methods of foreign banking contact and designate it as the
best form for every situation. The correspondent method
is the best for the majority of foreign banking operations because with most foreign points the volume of business transacted by any one bank is not sufficient to support a branch.
But where a bank carries on large operations with a foreign
center, especially in the neutral markets like South America
and the Orient, the branch will possess undeniable advantages
over the correspondent, and the branch will be installed unless
special considerations, such as those mentioned (pp. 29–35),
lead the bank to create a commandite or foreign subsidiary in
the foreign center or to establish a foreign branch of its
domestic subsidiary there.

The advantages possessed by the branch bank as over the
correspondent in the financing of foreign trade may be discussed under six major heads.

Responsibility to Clients

Complete Responsibility in the Branch Method.—Where
a bank has operated through a foreign correspondent and
difficulties occur in collecting or in any other phase of the
operation, the bank has often had to advise the American
exporter that it could not assume any responsibility for the
action of its correspondent, having over it no real control.
When the American exporter's draft against his shipment
of goods is sent by his bank in New York to its foreign correspondent, the shipper and his bank may expect that the
correspondent will make the collection in due form. Sometimes the expectations are not realized. The difficulties and
hardships experienced by American exporters and manufacturers due to the use of correspondent banks, states G. B.
Sherwell of the Department of Commerce.

. . . are very numerous and it would take a large space to enumerate the most important. They may, however, be summarized under two heads: poor and unreliable credit information, and most unsatisfactory collection service. Credit information obtained from foreign correspondents is often incomplete and in many cases unreliable. Some institutions in small places in foreign lands are not any too scrupulous in giving out information of this sort for fear of losing a client. As regards collection service, in innumerable instances losses to American exporters might have been avoided had the local banker abroad, who was supposed to take care of the exporter's interests in a proper manner, given the exporter the necessary data on local requirements, and a little advice perhaps.[1]

If a correspondent bank fail for any reason to execute the transaction entrusted to it in a satisfactory manner the American bank has to decline any responsibility for the failure of this correspondent, but if the bank operate through its foreign branch bank the responsibility to the client is continuous for the branch is legally an integral part of the parent institution.

Divided Responsibility in the Correspondent Method.— During the discussion on the responsibility of banks for the acts, reliability and performance of their correspondents at the National Foreign Trade Convention of 1924, W. H. Knox, representing the Merchants Association of New York, stated he could give . . . "a score of instances where an American bank has taken advantage of that clause which makes it not responsible for the acts of its agents."[2] Mr. Clifford, vice-president of the First National Bank of Chicago, replying to questions upon this subject said:

It is obvious that banks can be responsible only for the acts of agents over whom they have control. In the case of foreign banks, the local bank has no means of enforcing its instructions, and it would be an unfair burden to compel the domestic bank to undertake the control of people often thousands of miles away. All that a bank

---

[1] *Journal* of the American Bankers Association, October, 1922.

[2] Report of National Foreign Trade Convention, 1924, p. 101.

can be expected to do is to use due care in the selection of its agents and change agents who do not adhere strictly to instructions and international law.

It would not appear sound banking to assume responsibility for acts of agents of world wide scope amendable to such diversified laws and customs as to preclude in many instances the possibility of recourse.[3]

In speaking before the National Foreign Trade Convention of 1919, John E. Gardin, then Chairman of the International Banking Corporation, touched upon the responsibility of correspondents and branches:

Many of you have noted, when you handed your collections into the bank that you were told that the bank would assume no responsibility for any act of its agents over whom it had no control. So that if a failure took place while an item was in process of collection, and it just happened to strike you, and your check that was remitted was worthless, you were the sufferer. Your bank assumed no responsibility. Now that has been done away with.

Today responsibility is continuous [due to the employment of branches]. It is an item that really is worth consideration when you take into account the unknown quantity that you formerly had to employ in foreign business.[4]

In connection with this question of responsibility it appears logical that an exporter should prefer to deal with some bank in his locality which has a branch in the foreign market to which he ships his goods, for, as Dufourcq-Lagelouse, a French writer, says:

If difficulties arise he has in front of him only one banker near his residence against whom he can, if necessary, bring legal action, and not a foreign correspondent more or less unknown in a distant market where the laws and customs may be different. Thus the debts and credits rising from dealings with the banker run no risk of being subrogated.[5]

---

[3] Report of National Foreign Trade Convention, 1924, pp. 94–97.
[4] *Ibid.*, 1919, p. 204.
[5] L. Dufourcq-Lagelouse, Banques Étrangères en France, p. 81.

As early as 1903, W. L. Moyer, then president of the Mechanics and Traders Bank of New York, urged the establishment of American foreign branch banks on account of the continuous and full responsibility of the branch method as contrasted with the divided responsibility in foreign commercial banking through correspondents, stating,

No foreign bank can handle our foreign business satisfactorily in a distant land. Our banks, through foreign branches or agencies, must be able to follow our foreign trade through all its wanderings from factory to market. If a bank do less than this, it will satisfy neither its customers nor its stockholders.[6]

Protection and Care of Merchandise

Responsibility for Protection of Merchandise.—The protection of merchandise is included in the responsibility of a bank for the efficient execution of the foreign banking operations entrusted to it by its customers. The American who ships consignments abroad is primarily interested in their prompt and full payment. He prefers, when possible, to bill his goods "Documents against Acceptance" which means that the foreign importer cannot secure possession of the shipment until he has accepted the draft drawn upon him for the full amount of the goods,[7] or "Documents against Payment," in which case the importer must pay for the consignment before taking possession of it.

In these ways the exporter may endeavor to make certain that his goods will be paid for. However, in some countries the law does not sufficiently protect the interests of the foreign exporter who ships in merchandise. Merchants in such countries have often secured possession of goods shipped to them without payment but by a simple declaration that the articles were consigned to them even though the goods had

---

[6] An address before the Missouri Bankers' Association at St. Louis, May, 1903, cited by W. H. Hull in Practical Problems in Banking and Currency, p. 18.

[7] When he writes across the face of the draft "accepted" and signs his name, he obligates himself to pay the full amount of the draft at the place and on the date stated on the instrument.

been billed "Documents against Payment." In Brazil, Venezuela, and Colombia, for example, importers were able under domestic law to secure merchandise without payment or acceptance. P. L. Bell, reporting to the United States Bureau of Commerce in 1922 on Venezuela, remarked:

"To order" shipments cannot be made to Venezuela because the possession of the bill of lading is no guarantee of payment for merchandise, the existing laws allowing delivery to be obtained by the holder of the consular invoice, or copy of such invoice which may be procured from the customs authorities at the port of entry upon a small payment by the person whose name appears on the original.

In order to obviate this difficulty and to furnish protection to American exporters, the American Mercantile Bank of Caracas has established a branch at La Guaira . . . and delivers the merchandise to the importer only against payment or acceptance of the draft or as otherwise specially instructed.[8]

The protection of consignments exported from the United States could only be provided for effectively in many cases by the establishment of American foreign branch banks. In some countries of South America, of the Orient, and even of Europe the laws have not protected the interests of American exporters, and foreign branches of our banks have been necessary to insure such protection. The advantage of the branch over the correspondent is clear here. When the foreign shipment of an American manufacturer or merchant is financed by an American bank having a branch in the country of the importer, the branch can intervene and take care that no irregularities occur in the delivery of the goods. In actual practice American foreign branch banks showed their usefulness early in this matter, Mr. Gardin, stating at the Sixth National Foreign Trade Convention, "Since we have had branch banks in South America I cannot recall a single instance where merchants have lost anything through the delivery of goods without proper authority." [9]

---

[8] Special Agents Series No. 212, pp. 167–168.
[9] Report of the National Foreign Trade Convention, 1919, p. 205.

Care of Merchandise.—The branch bank not only protects the merchandise of its clients but it is sometimes called upon to perform two other functions in connection with the care of shipments of goods. The first has to do with disposing of shipments refused by foreign importers. When a cargo shipped by an American exporter to a foreigner is refused by the latter the exporter must depend largely upon the bank in the importer's country which is handling that end of the transaction to make the best possible arrangement for the disposal of the goods. When the bank in question is the branch of an American institution it is obvious that the American exporter's interests are better looked after than in the case where the bank is a native establishment or the branch of a foreign bank acting as correspondent. Refusals of American goods were especially numerous following the World Crisis of 1920, and American foreign branch banks rendered important services to our exporters in arranging for the disposal of the refused shipments.

The Branch as a Mercantile Agency.—The second service relates to the functioning of the branch as a mercantile agency. By this it is meant that the branch bank sometimes acts as an agent for its home exporters and importers, receiving goods for sale and acting as a purchasing agent. The branch may also act as a purchasing agent for foreigners wishing to import goods from the United States. Some banks having branches abroad have been unwilling to act in this capacity of mercantile agent, while others have performed the service in special cases if not as a general rule.

Protection of Trade Secrets

Question of the Necessity for Protecting Trade Secrets.— The necessity for protecting trade secrets by the use of branch banks abroad has been much discussed, especially since the

World War. It is logical that a bank should favor the commerce of its countrymen as much as possible, but it is difficult to believe that a bank would violate the secrets of its foreign clients to accomplish this. However, foreign banks have been widely criticized on this score, it being claimed that, in handling business for American merchants, they have given copies of invoices and bills of lading and information upon costs of production, prices, and other trade secrets to the business men of their own countries. Some typical statements of American manufacturers interested in foreign trade and of well-known students of banking follow.

If we had to deal, for instance, through a —— bank, we felt that practically everything that occurred in regard to our transaction which could be found out from the outside was known to our competitors when the next time came. The amount of money that we paid for our locomotives was known to that bank to the last dollar. . . . They often knew all that we paid for freight and everything of that kind, and we felt that at times we saw the evidence of that knowledge when it came to the next bidding.[10]

Never an invoice nor bill of lading came into their hands but that it was copied and sent to their home office and there made use of to the fullest extent.[11]

The fact that invoices, bills of lading and other documents passed through the hands of foreign banks and of South American or Oriental branches of foreign banks gave to our foreign competitors "inside" information concerning our foreign business,—information that was often used to their advantage in competition with our own citizens.[12]

Where as in the South American trade it has been necessary for the American business man to resort to branches of European banks established in the various countries, it has been asserted that such banks, working as they did in close harmony with the merchants of their own nationality, were often unfaithful to their American clients,

---

[10] Testimony of the president of the American Locomotive Company in Co-operation in American Export Trade, Vol. II, p. 313.

[11] Report of the National Foreign Trade Convention, 1919, p. 204.

[12] E. W. Kemmerer, A. B. C. of the Federal Reserve System, p. 24.

allowing competitors to know their business operations, and when disposed to do so, cutting off their credit in favor of such rivals.

These charges have more or less foundation, and it has certainly been true that the banking accommodations of Americans engaged in foreign operations have been poor even at the best.[13]

Foreign banks, under the control and devoted primarily to the welfare of foreign industry, could not be expected to perform all these services with strict secrecy and impartiality. It was a matter of comment that American trade secrets found frequent disclosure through the medium of foreign banks.[14]

A manufacturer of glazed kid says that foreign banks often use the information which they procure through invoices and bills of lading to the advantage of the foreign competitors.

Conclusive proof of such allegations is hard to obtain and none has been sought by the Commission. Statements like the foregoing, however, represent a widespread belief.[15]

Belief in the Betrayal of Trade Secrets a Motive for Foreign Branch Bank Expansion.—In discussing the advantages of branch banks in connection with this subject of protection of trade secrets two points may be made. In the first place, although the abuses of the confidence of American exporters by foreign banks have no doubt been greatly overexaggerated yet it is certainly true that a belief in the advantage of the branch bank as a protector of trade secrets has constituted one of the motives for the establishment of American foreign branch banks. Here, where we are engaged in explaining why American foreign branch banks were established, it does not necessarily matter whether there were many or no violations of American trade secrets by foreign banks. The important fact is that the conviction was widespread that foreign banks were unfaithful to their American clients. It was felt that reliance upon foreign banks and branches of foreign banks acting as correspondents placed Americans in a position

---

[13] H. P. Willis, American Banking, p. 292.
[14] H. L. Reed, Development of Federal Reserve Policy, p. 176.
[15] Co-operation in American Export Trade, Vol. I, p. 61.

of dependency and weakness and the establishment of foreign branches of American banks was urged.

Control of Export Businesses by Banks.—Secondly, it may be stated that under certain conditions a bank may indeed be tempted to reveal trade secrets of foreign clients to its native merchants. In the case of banks owning partial or entire control of industrial and mercantile enterprises doing a foreign business the banks may quite conceivably be led to disclose secrets of foreign competitors to the concerns in which these banks have interests. Such examples have not been lacking in certain quarters. Were a tendency to develop generally in foreign countries for banks to acquire interests in export businesses the advantage claimed for branch banks as protectors of the secrets of our foreign traders would permit of no argument.

Information Service

Importance of Good Information Service.—Accurate and timely information upon the economic and political conditions, upon the demand and supply of certain goods in the various foreign markets, and upon the credit standing of prospective clients is of the utmost importance to the business man who engages in foreign trade. A bank obtains some such information from its correspondents but it is through a system of branch banks that an institution receives the best and most complete credit and commercial information.

No correspondent can be as active in informing an American bank as the bank's own foreign branch nor will as accurate, thorough, and extensive information be secured from correspondents as from a net of foreign branch banks. The information received by a bank from its branches is complete for if at any time the bank feels that its file on any subject or country is lacking it may order a special investigation made by the branch or branches concerned; but a foreign correspondent cannot be ordered to perform a service by an American bank.

Branch Banks and Credit Information.—In treating the subject of credit information, Magee cites the survey made by the Federal Reserve Board:

> It is, however, the general belief that credit data given by American banks are by far more reliable and valuable than information furnished by foreign banks. The following answers from two large firms engaged in foreign trade express the general opinion of American business houses with regard to information given by banking institutions: "We consider the most reliable information received is that secured from American overseas banks or foreign branches of American banks." "We think the best information is obtained from banks in this country who have foreign branches or who are in a position to secure information from other banks." [16]

The reports of the special agents sent out by the United States Department of Commerce to study conditions abroad in the interest of American foreign trade are valuable to us in that they are prepared by experts who through investigations in foreign countries secure first hand knowledge. In reporting to the Department of Commerce in 1919 on Brazil, Hurley mentions the credit information service of foreign banks to Americans:

> It is not to be expected that in the campaign for Brazilian trade foreign banks will give credit information as readily to American concerns as to traders of their own nationality. Americans can and do obtain credit information from foreign banks in South America, but as a rule its possession results in no material stimulation of competition.
>
> If an American lumber or flour company asks a German or British bank for financial rating of a certain Brazilian client or for specific information regarding the condition of his business, the bank may readily comply, for the resulting sales in lumber or flour are non-competitive. It is doubtful if inquiries preliminary to a transaction in competitive manufactures would be so readily answered.

---

[16] J. D. Magee, Materials for the Study of Banking, p. 682.

Credit information is a prime banking asset in Brazil acquired only by timely, painstaking and long-continued effort. No financial institution may be expected to part with it to occasional clients. Of course, where an American firm is an old and profitable client of a foreign bank in Brazil, it may have access to credit information on the same basis as customers of the same nationality as the bank. But, however convenient such an arrangement may appear, it possesses inherent weakness.[17]

After the passage of the Federal Reserve Act several American banks entered the South American market, and we read in a Special Agents Report submitted to the Department of Commerce in 1921,

One of the most valuable services rendered by these branches to American exporters is in furnishing more and more accurate credit information, many large American exporters having reported this service as being extremely helpful and entirely adequate.[18]

Branch Banks and Commercial Information.—For commercial information as well as for credit information the branch bank is of far greater service to the home institution than a correspondent for it is always awake and alert, looking for opportunities which may be turned to profit by the parent bank. The branch bank takes the initiative in informing the home office on everything of possible interest in the market where it is located, while a bank acting as correspondent cannot render such service to its thousands of correspondents.

The files of the great banks having branches abroad are always complete and carefully kept up to date. These banks make a specialty of commercial information; their branches, working in close and efficient harmony with them, keep their foreign trade departments posted upon trade and exchange possibilities all over the world. The National City Bank of New York, as a result of the investigations carried on by its branches, receives a continuous flow of information which is

---

[17] Special Agents Series, No. 90, pp. 11, 46, 47.
[18] Ibid., No. 206, p. 334.

sent to the home office in the form of *Commercial Reports* on trade concerns, *Industrial Reports* on manufacturing establishments, *Trade Reports* on commodities, and *Miscellaneous Reports* on various subjects: customs and tariff changes, trade mark laws, public works, etc.   Beside these regular reports special information on specific trade opportunities and commercial matters is received upon request.   The branches of this bank have "special representatives who devote their time to studying trade conditions and searching for new prospects and business opportunities in their particular districts." [19]   The bank distributes the information received from its branches through its weekly bulletin "Foreign Trade Opportunities," by direct replies to letters of inquiry, and by interviews.

When a client of the bank goes abroad he is advised on all matters of interest to his business by the foreign department of the home office in New York City and given letters of introduction to the bank's foreign branches which offer him all their facilities and aid him in every way when he arrives.

Superiority of the Branch over the Correspondent.— French banks, like American institutions until these last few years, have been slow to expand abroad, and consequently one finds authors on economic subjects in that country urging the necessity of foreign branch banks.   One of them, Berrogain, has no doubt as to the desirability of branch banks in foreign countries, and says upon the subject of commercial information from branches:

Besides the normal banking operations with which they are charged, they send regularly to the home office reports on the commercial situation of the region, the industrial movement, prospects to be considered, and in general on all the questions of commercial, agricultural, industrial and financial interest.

---

[19] Langston, L. H., Practical Bank Operation, Vol. II, pp. 667, 692: "New business prospects come to the attention of the bank in a variety of ways.   The most important agencies for seeking out desirable customers are branches of the bank and the domestic field men."

The result is a file of information at the home office which is always up-to-date and which permits the bank to advise its clientele, either to restrain it in threatening periods or to indicate possible markets.[20]

As to the commercial information service of foreign banks acting as correspondents he states:

A foreign bank does not furnish and cannot furnish to our merchants information susceptible of permitting them to extend their business at the expense of the nationals of the foreign bank. Can we really expect that a foreign bank will inform us that such and such a market could be easily worked by French exportation? If the foreign banks facilitate French trade in its present state it would be puerile to expect of them an active rôle in its expansion.[21]

The American experience with foreign branch banks has demonstrated that their employment means better commercial information. J. C. Muniz, acting consul general for Brazil, in referring to American branch banks in a speech before the Pan-American Commercial Congress of 1925, declared:

American co-operation in the development of South American countries has increased greatly in the last few years. Among the factors bringing about these closer relations was the establishment of American banks in South America, made possible by the Federal Reserve Board. Trade relations between our countries, particularly in regard to credit, were greatly hampered before because the financing of American exports to South America had to be done by London banks.

With the establishment of branches of American banks in South America, the direct transactions which ensued were productive of better knowledge of the conditions and necessities of our markets.[22]

Information Service Mutually Valuable to Client and Bank.—A highly developed commercial and credit information service is not only of great value to the clients of a bank, but it is of the very first importance to the bank itself if it wishes to

---

[20] Berrogain, Expansion du Commerce Extérieur, p. 38.
[21] *Ibid.*, p. 89.
[22] *Wall Street Journal*, December 24, 1925.

engage safely in a large volume of operations.   The value of foreign branches to the great bank is emphasized by Lucien Dufourcq-Lagelouse of the Banque Française-Italienne at Paris:

> The necessity of being constantly informed, of knowing at every moment the extent of the risk run in this or that operation and the events susceptible of changing the situation,—all that renders indispensable an organization which even intimate relations with a correspondent can only with difficulty replace.[23]

Export Financing.—In the financing of both exports and imports the risk may be materially reduced by the activity of the bank's foreign branches in gathering information for it. When an American exporter ships goods to a foreign country and draws a commercial draft upon the importer he may wish to realize upon the draft by: (1) having an American bank take it as security and allowing him to draw a draft to be accepted by the bank and sold forthwith in the market; (2) having the bank buy the commercial draft outright, with or without recourse, depending upon the credit standing of the foreign drawee; (3) having the bank take the commercial draft as collateral for a loan.   If the bank has a branch in the foreign importer's country it can obtain accurate and up-to-date information upon his credit standing and upon general conditions in the country and deal with the matter in hand without unnecessary risk.   If it does not have trustworthy information it will either assume an unknown risk or refuse to grant the American exporter as good terms as the case would really justify.

Import Financing.—In financing American imports or trade between foreign countries the American bank with foreign branches can with safety grant acceptances freely in favor of foreigners when requested to do so by its foreign branches.

---

[23] L. Dufourcq-Lagelouse, *op. cit.*, p. 80.

These branches are in the best possible position for investigating the credit standing of their clients for whom they make such requests, and the home bank is thus able to handle with safety a great volume of bills having unknown foreign names. The information furnished by branches upon the social, economic and political conditions in the countries where they are located also permits the parent bank to avoid risk by enabling it to know when and where to restrict or extend credit. The general conditions of a foreign market must be taken into consideration as well as the credit standing of the client, and any untoward trend in these conditions must be given careful attention in directing the granting of credits.

From the viewpoints of both bank and foreign trader, the excellent commercial and credit information service of branch banks constitutes one of their chief points of superiority over other forms of banking contact with foreign markets, and even those who are lukewarm to the idea of foreign branch banking must agree with Moulton that,

> While the advantages of developing branches of American banks in foreign countries have no doubt been greatly exaggerated, it is nevertheless true that expansion of our foreign trade would be expedited in some degree by the development of American banking facilities abroad. The intimate association of the branch bank managers with business men and importers in foreign countries, together with the acquisition of knowledge on the part of American bankers of the credit standing of foreign buyers, are matters of first importance in developing overseas trade and will no doubt improve our opportunities for a lucrative expansion of our foreign business.[24]

Cost of Financing Foreign Trade

Possibility of Reducing the Cost of Financing.—In addition to providing more efficient and responsible execution of banking operations for our foreign trade, more thorough protection to American exporters, and a superior information

---

[24] H. G. Moulton, Financial Organization, pp. 421–422.

service, American banks working through foreign branches are in many cases able to finance foreign shipments entrusted to them for a smaller commission than that charged by a bank operating through a correspondent. In the foreign trade financed by a bank and its correspondent, two regular commissions are taken by the two banks. But a bank operating through its branch can take a somewhat smaller total commission if it is really out to get business. In practice this has been the policy of American banks having foreign branches, and "as lower collection commissions are charged between head offices and branches than when dealing with correspondents abroad, such expense to the merchants can be properly reduced." [25]

American Branch Banks as Supporters of Dollar Exchange.—It is also argued that American branch banks abroad help to reduce the cost of financing our foreign trade in that they are valuable supporters of dollar exchange. Two questions suggest themselves here. Is financing by dollar exchange inherently cheaper than financing by sterling or other exchange? If dollar exchange possess any advantages over other exchange, are American branch banks abroad of any importance in giving support to the market for dollar exchange? Whether dollar exchange be cheaper than other exchange depends mostly upon whether discount rates are lower in New York than in foreign financial centers. In this particular London may regain some day its old advantage over New York.

Although the primacy of the sterling bill before the war and the importance of the dollar bill of exchange today may be mainly explained as a matter of discount rates, something must be said in regard to the support given by foreign branch banks to a bill.

By actively buying and selling bills on New York, American foreign branch banks lead the importers of the countries where they are located to accept willingly drafts in dollars

---

[25] A. B. Cook, Financing Exports and Imports, p. 176.

drawn upon them by American exporters. In this way the American exporter can draw in dollars instead of in a foreign currency, a direct operation taking the place of the triangular transaction necessitated when he draws in a foreign money, with a consequent reduction in the expense of commissions. Moreover, since he draws in dollars he does not run the risk of exchange and can thus quote the lowest possible price to his foreign prospect. More certainty is given in this way to American exporting by the existence of American foreign branch banks and the cost of foreign banking operations tends to be lowered with the result that both American banks and foreign trade benefit. American importing benefits in like manner from the support given to dollar exchange by American foreign branch banks in that in many cases foreigners exporting to America will draw directly in dollars on some great American bank instead of drawing the drafts in a foreign currency.

The advantage accruing to American merchants engaged in foreign trade is well stated by Filsinger:

One of the direct results of the establishment of branch banks in accordance with the provisions of the recently enacted Federal Reserve Act will be the creation of a permanent market for dollar exchange. As the branch banks will be branches of powerful American institutions, they will be enabled to sell drafts in dollars on the head institution. As a result, at least one of the commissions which merchants have heretofore had to pay in the form of a collection charge on a London bank will be wiped out, and the value of the dollar in international banking will be definitely established.

Furthermore, the advantage to purchasers of such bills is a saving of interest for 10 or 12 days; the commission is also more reasonable than in the past and the risk of fluctuations in the exchange is eliminated. The influence of this method of doing business will be of phenomenal importance.[26]

Some students place great emphasis upon the support rendered to the market for dollar exchange by American foreign branch banks. For example:

---

[26] E. B. Filsinger, Exporting to Latin America, p. 218.

If the dollar draft were to acquire a permanent position, American banks would of necessity be forced to establish foreign branches through which American capital could be exported, and which would be in a position to secure credit information for exporters and in other ways look after their interests. The English banks and English-controlled banks, with their thousands of branches in all parts of the world, had been an important factor in contributing to the primacy of the sterling bill.[27]

The latter author quoted does not claim that the foreign branches of English banks were the most important factor or the only factor in the primacy of the sterling bill, nor does the preceding writer's thesis argue that American foreign branch banks would alone assure an important market for dollar exchange. They simply call attention to the fact that American and English foreign branch banks contribute to the support of the dollar and sterling bills of exchange.

The Question of Discrimination.—Still the question arises, why should American foreign branch banks be urged in this connection when there are great numbers of branches of foreign banks scattered all over the world? Here some students argue that branches of foreign banks will many times buy and sell the exchange of their own countries at more favorable rates than other exchange (dollar exchange, for example), and thus influence the position of the dollar bill of exchange and the flow of trade in a manner unwelcome to American interests. For example, it is stated that,

To assist the trade of England, an English branch bank will buy sterling at a more favorable rate than dollars, and it will refuse to open a dollar credit for the importer who is buying merchandise from the United States that he could equally well purchase from England.

The inability to purchase and sell exchange on New York with facility has often been the deciding factor in securing for our competitors trade that might otherwise have come to the United States.[28]

---

[27] B. H. Beckhardt, Discount Policy of the Federal Reserve System, p. 234.
[28] Course in Foreign Trade, pp. 62–3.

In South American countries and other markets where American and European interests are active competitors, branch banks are often able to influence the flow of local business by their quotations on exchange. In the absence of American banks, rates as quoted by other banks, particularly banks of competing countries may be so unfavorable that local merchants will prefer to do their foreign business in other currencies than dollar exchange. It may, therefore, be argued that American branches are needed to hold the trade won since 1914.[29]

If instances are found where foreign institutions give better quotations in buying and selling exchange on their native lands than on the United States, the discount rates in foreign centers and in New York being the same, one is not necessarily forced to make charges of narrow nationalism on the part of the foreign institutions. Instead, one may venture the explanation presented by officers of branch banking establishments that, if the foreign institution in question is the branch of an English bank it means that its funds are borrowed in London and, therefore, it is naturally desirous of buying bills of exchange on that center to meet its obligations and build up its account there. Also when it has an opportunity to sell bills on a foreign center it may prefer to sell bills on London for that is where it has built up its balance. Thus it appears quite natural that branches of English, German, French and American banks may often make a little better rate on bills drawn on London, Berlin, Paris and New York respectively.

As to American foreign branch banks and the market for dollar exchange, Cook states:

With the advent of the American branch bank in South America, Cuba, and an increase in the same facilities in the Orient, purchasers for dollar drafts thus appeared in the exchange markets of these countries who were eager to get business and would consequently pay a little more of local currency to exporters for drafts on this country. American bankers in those foreign markets also sold New York exchange at a slightly better figure, usually, to local importers, thus

[29] G. W. Edwards, International Trade Finance, pp. 177–8.

stabilizing to a considerable degree trading in the exchange and preventing local bankers and foreign branches of European institutions from favoring sterling, francs, lire, etc., at the expense of the dollar. [30]

In leaving this topic it may be said that during the past ten years discount rates in New York relative to those in foreign centers have been such that American bank acceptances have been chosen to finance a large part of our foreign trade, and that American foreign branch banks have contributed appreciable support to the market for dollar exchange. When New York rates are as favorable as those in foreign centers the use of the American branch bank and American bank acceptances removes the risk of exchange encountered when using acceptances of foreign banks, and it makes possible lower commissions and lower total costs.

Psychological Motives

Natural Preference of a People for the Services of its Own Banks.—Any discussion of the rôle played by the branch bank in financing the foreign trade of a nation would be incomplete were the psychological motives affecting the establishment of branches disregarded. For it is certain that the preference of individuals for the services of banks run by their countrymen has been one of the causes of the expansion of branch banks abroad. A business man dealing with customers in foreign markets likes to have his operations financed and taken care of by a bank run by his own fellow citizens. If he be an American, he wants his business handled according to American business methods to which he is accustomed and which he considers superior to all others. He wants his affairs transacted by bankers who understand his personality.

The bank which carries on its foreign operations through a foreign institution acting as its correspondent cannot satisfy

---

[30] A. B. Cook, *op. cit.*, p. 143.

this natural desire of the American business man. Langston puts it very well when he says,

One of the primary objects attained in a branch bank is a real, live attention to the needs of American interests in the foreign field. It is felt by many that in dealing with most countries the branch bank system has an advantage over the correspondent banking method of transacting international banking business, in that the branch bank has the American viewpoint of the foreign field and is therefore primarily the servant of the American business man.[31]

Better Understanding of American Trade Requirements by American Banks.—At the National Foreign Trade Convention of 1924, the Special Committee reporting on American foreign trade policy expressed the desire of American business men interested in foreign commerce in the following words:

It is only natural that American traders abroad should encounter a little more sympathetic service at the hands of the branches or agencies of American financial institutions than they would from those of foreign concerns. It is only natural that there should be on the part of such branches or agencies a little better understanding of the conditions and requirements of American trade than would be found in foreign institutions. It is only natural also that there should be on the part of such American financial institutions abroad a greater and more whole hearted desire to assist in upbuilding of American commerce than there is on the part of foreign concerns. . . . . We do not suggest that American banks should go abroad and stay on a permanently losing basis. But we do suggest the importance of taking advantage of every opportunity to extend their service to the benefit of our trade.[32]

The preference of people for the services of their countrymen is a very definite fact all over the world, and, as far as it concerns the expansion of American foreign branch banks, it has had its full effect due to the enormous amount of foreign trade and travel done by Americans since the war, and to the

---

[31] L. H. Langston, *op. cit.*, Vol. II, p. 666.
[32] Report of the National Foreign Trade Convention, 1924, p. 187.

unwillingness on the part of Americans to adapt themselves to any other methods of business than their own.

In the advertisement quoted below a great American bank presents some of the advantages of an American foreign branch bank to American foreign traders and starts out with an appeal to what we have called the psychological motive.

How Can Your Foreign Offices Help Me?

By carrying an interest-bearing account with either the Paris or London Office of The Equitable you may—

1. Enjoy the advantages of an American bank, employing American methods, in the handling of your foreign business.

2. Pay foreign bills by check, thus effecting a saving in interest, or you may arrange with us to pay your commissionnaire upon presentation of certain shipping documents.

3. Estimate import costs on a definite exchange basis, thus eliminating the speculation involved in meeting obligations at a future date.

4. Buy exchange to replenish your balance when you consider rates to be most favorable.

5. Establish a valuable local reference overseas.

6. Secure first-hand trade and credit information.

7. Save your traveling representatives time and trouble through the Foreign Travel Service of our Paris Office.

CHAPTER IV

BRANCH BANKS AND THE PROMOTION OF FOREIGN TRADE

Branch Banks for Active Promotion of Foreign Trade.—
A nation may, if it so chooses, rely entirely upon foreign banks
for the financing of its foreign commerce. Branch banks are
not absolutely necessary for the mere financing of a country's
trade, but for the active promotion of a nation's trade in all
parts of the world branch banks have advantages. Foreign
banks acting as correspondents do not "promote" our foreign
trade, for by promotion is meant that definite and conscious im-
pulsion given to the foreign trade of a nation by its banks
which follow a policy of furthering the international trade of
their countrymen with more energy than that which they devote to the interests of the nationals of any other country.[1]
This nationalistic co-operation is a fact to be reckoned with in
discussing foreign trade expansion.

Nationalistic Co-operation

**Nationalistic Co-operation Between Banker and Foreign
Trader.—**It is characteristic of the expansion of banking organizations for the financing of foreign trade that the banks
of the great nations have adopted policies which have for their
principal object the furtherance of the trade interests of their
own nationals as opposed to those of foreign competitors. The
results of these policies have been especially evident in the

---

[1] "Hundreds of specific instances could be cited where our American banks established in foreign cities have directly fostered trade," A. A. Preciado, Exporting to the
World, p. 311.

competition by the business interests of the great powers for the trade of non-European countries.

German Banks and German Foreign Trade.—The German banks from the very first accepted as their duty the task of promoting German trade. The great German bank, the Deutsche Bank, which was the leader in developing German foreign trade, stated in paragraph two of its charter,

> The object of the company is the transaction of all sorts of banking business, particularly the fostering and facilitating of commercial relations between Germany, the other European countries, and oversea markets.

This was the first formulation of a policy of active promotion of German trade which was adopted by the great German banks.[2] Riesser, who has written perhaps the best account of the development of the great banking establishments of Germany, says in connection with this policy,

> The German banks regarded it as one of their chief functions actively to support, both at home and abroad, domestic industry and the export policy adopted by it by promoting energetically German foreign commerce.
>
> In connection with this general policy they came to establish branches in foreign countries, and to organize for the foreign business special subsidiary banks both at home and abroad, which, it is true, in many cases proved at the same time the means of securing new and profitable business.[3]

Before 1870 German trade, just like American trade up to 1914, was financed by foreign banks under the correspondent method, and this was decidedly unsatisfactory to the industrial and commercial interests of a nation which wished to expand its foreign trade in the most effective way. German branch

---

[1] "In all its activities abroad the Deutsche Bank was governed by the viewpoint . . . . 'Die politischen Vorpostengefechte werden auf finanziellen Boden geschlagen' (the skirmishes of the political advance posts are fought out on financial ground). This is shown best by the bank's activities in Turkey, in the case of the Anatolian and the Bagdad railroads, etc." Riesser, *op. cit.*, p. 474.

[2] *Ibid.*, p. 529.

banks abroad were felt to be necessary as the most efficient means of promoting the nation's foreign trade, and,

> As soon as German trade felt certain of banking support in its import and export activity on the part of the branches of the banks in the great centers of overseas trade, or of the German subsidiary banks working hand in hand with the parent banks in Germany, it naturally emancipated itself from the foreign intermediaries by enlisting the usually much cheaper services of the German banks and their branches or of their subsidiary banks.[4]

Illustrations from Holland, Japan, and Canada.—But German banks were not exceptions in their policy of favoring the foreign trade of their nationals. The policy of nationalistic co-operation between merchant and banker in the exploitation of foreign markets has been general.[5] In Holland we find in Article 65 of the original charter of the Nederlandsche Handel-Maatschappij, issued on August 18, 1824, that,

> The object of the Society is the promotion of national trade, shipping, shipbuilding, fisheries, agriculture, factories, and transport by means of extending, with due observance of its own interests, the commercial connections at present existing and which are advantageous for the Netherlands, by opening up new avenues for Dutch commerce, and by means of such enterprises as can promote and increase the activity of Netherlands industry.[6]

In Japan, the Yokohama Specie Bank was founded in 1880 for promoting the country's foreign trade. Japanese financial writers give much credit to the Yokohama Specie Bank for the growth of Japanese commerce. "It is scarcely

---

[4] Riesser, *op. cit.*, p. 425. Riesser says, "German trade . . . emancipated itself from the foreign intermediaries." It did emancipate itself to a great extent but far from completely, for as late as 1914 London was financing as much of Germany's foreign trade as Berlin. Thus far it appears that American foreign trade "emancipation" has been proceeding as successfully as did the German, due to favorable rates of discount in New York. That German banks did help German foreign trade and that American banks have helped American foreign commerce cannot be denied.

[5] "There has been a decided tendency on the part of some foreign banks to withhold credit information from manufacturers with whom they have no business relations or sympathies especially if they belong to a nation that is trying to break in on the trade of the countries with which the banks are affiliated." L. and T. Ford, Foreign Trade of the United States, p. 193.

[6] *Bankers Magazine*, May, 1925, p. 939.

necessary to dwell upon the fact," says the *Japan Financial and Economic Monthly,* "that the development of foreign trade is attributable to this banking organization." [7]   The banks of Canada, it is said, pursue a policy of patriotically promoting the country's foreign trade.   H. M. P. Eckardt, for 19 years in a great Canadian bank, writes about Canadian foreign branch banks as follows:

> One may well understand that these agencies, wherever they exist, are potential factors in building up Canada's foreign trade, in extending her good name, and attracting capital to the Dominion, while at the same time doing useful service in discovering profitable investments abroad for Canadian capital.
>
> No matter in what forms the commercial and productive activity of these foreign peoples finds expression, the men in the Canadian branches are certain to be thoroughly informed about the whole. Loyalty to Canada, to the banks employing them, and to the localities in which they are situated impels them to open new channels of trade with the Dominion when such a course is likely to result in natural profit for the trading nations.[8]

Promotion of Trade in South America by Branch Banks.— A South American economist, Guillermo Subercaseaux, in his "Monetary and Banking Policy of Chile," remarks how German banks have favored German interests and English banks promoted British interests in his home country, and sees a greater growth of American trade with South America due to the establishment of branches of large American banks.   He states:

> The German banks have greatly facilitated commercial negotiations between Germany and Chile, and at the same time have greatly favored the development of certain German enterprises organized in Chile. . . .   The English banks have likewise rendered very valuable services in the development of the commercial relations of Chile and Great Britain.
>
> This institution (the National City Bank of New York) is destined

---

[7] Issue of March, 1915, p. 45.
[8] H. M. P. Eckardt, A Rational Banking System, pp. 265-266.

to do much toward developing the commercial relations between the United States and the Republics of South America. A well-managed bank, such as this one must necessarily be, may promote Pan-American trade in a truly extraordinary manner.

If, for example, a merchant or manufacturer residing in Chile, and possessing no credit relations with the United States, has need of some foreign merchandise or has to manufacture some special kind of machinery, the National City Bank, subject to the procurement of the proper guarantees, will take charge of the order in the United States; and, having done this, it will transport the merchandise to Chile and deliver it to the merchant or manufacturer who placed the order.[9]

Were there no American branch bank in Chile, the business man in the above example would very likely place his order in Germany through the German branch bank or in England through the English branch. It is for this reason that American branch banks in foreign countries, and especially in the neutral markets, were urged for the advancement of American foreign trade.

Teamwork Between Banks and Business Men.—J. A. Fowler, reporting to the Department of Commerce in 1923 on Netherlands, East Indies and British Malaya, noted in connection with the principle of nationalistic co-operation that,

The large British commercial interests make the presence of these representative British banking institutions (the branches of the Hongkong and Shanghai Banking Corporation and other British banks) a matter of prime importance and their relations with the British mercantile houses are an object lesson in teamwork that might be studied with profit by not only American banks but by American manufacturers and exporters.[10]

The experience of the Deutsche Uberseeische Bank in Spain indicates the effectiveness of a branch bank in promoting its country's trade with its country of location.

---

[9] Guillermo Subercaseaux, Monetary and Banking Policy of Chile, pp. 134-135.
[10] Special Agents Series No. 218, p. 356. In regard to the International Banking Corporation's branches in Java: "This is the only American bank in this colony and its success here is very important to America's general commercial interests."

Before the war this bank was an important part of the German organization for furthering German commercial interests in Spain. These interests had made notable progress in the years prior to 1914, as indicated by the fact that Germany was first among the countries from which Spain imported manufactured articles. In 1913, 53% of the machinery and parts thereof imported into Spain came from Germany.[11]

American Branch Banks to Promote American Trade.— Writers on trade promotion, business men, and many economists were of the belief long before 1914 that although foreign banks could and did facilitate American foreign trade by giving information and opening credits, it was too much to expect that these foreign institutions would take an active interest in the foreign trade expansion of Americans in those cases where it meant competition against the houses of their own nationals. Consequently the establishment of American foreign branch banks was demanded to support actively our foreign commerce.

The experience of England and of Germany has shown the great advantage, not to say the necessity, of having in foreign countries, especially the great neutral markets like South America and the Orient, agencies of home banks or independent institutions established by home interests for the purpose of financing foreign trade. . . . We have depended for our foreign operations on alien bankers. This has involved heavy tribute to such bankers, and, since they have naturally favored the trade of their own country wherever they could, it has hindered the development of American foreign trade.[12]

The branches of English and German banks have faithfully adhered to the purpose for which they were founded, and have labored indefatigably and successfully to foster the trade of England and Germany. To expect that at the same time they would foster the trade of a large and powerful competitor would be unreasonable; the service, therefore, that they have rendered the United States has been purely perfunctory and devoid of any desire to further the interests of this country.[13]

---

[11] Special Agents Series, No. 202, p. 51.
[12] E. E. Agger, Organized Banking, p. 238.
[13] Course in Foreign Trade, pp. 64-5.

It was admitted that twenty-five years ago American foreign branch banks, were not greatly needed by our foreign trade for as an agricultural nation we did not compete with the great powers which were manufacturing nations. But the rise of the United States as an exporter of manufactured products was stressed and American foreign branch banks were deemed necessary in this new situation to give our merchants the same support as that received by their competitors.

So long as the United States was primarily an agricultural nation and did not compete with Europe in industrial markets, it was perfectly appropriate that we should accept the services of transportation and banking. The trade of each was complementary and there was a gain for both in economies from the use of the same intermediaries. As the United States becomes a competitor of Europe, however, trade ceases to be complementary and many of the economies disappear. Moreover, for a country to place itself at the mercy of its competitors would be absurd. Germany at first utilized the services of British banks and ships, but her commerce developed only when she had established her own banks abroad and built her own merchant marine.[14]

Foreign Investments, Foreign Trade and Foreign Branch Banks

Effect of Capital Export on Foreign Trade.—The export of capital by a nation influences both its foreign trade and its establishment of branch banks abroad. Some loans—a minority—are made with provisions that the proceeds are to be spent in the lending country, but most of them appear to be made without restrictions. This is especially true of foreign loans made by Americans. In the case where the borrowing country does not promise to spend the loan in the lending country, trade between the two countries may nevertheless be stimulated. Some writers hold that the sale of the securities advances the rate of exchange of the borrowing nation making

---

[14] A. W. Lahee, *Our Competitors and Markets*, p. 19.

it easier to place orders in the lending country. It is doubtful, others maintain, that the direct effect of lending operations on the rate of exchange generally has much to do with the matter. Many of the loans are spent in the first instance in the borrowing country (the case of many of our loans to Europe), and the reserves (gold and foreign exchange holdings) of the banks of the borrowing country are increased in the process. There may, therefore, be an expansion of domestic credit, which, together with the direct effect of the spending of the proceeds of the foreign loan, may lead to an increase of prices and hence an increase of imports—but only part of these may come from the lending country. If the loans be very large, prices may be decreased or made lower than otherwise they would have been in the lending country, thus making it a good market in which to buy.[15]

Control of Foreign Investments.—Sometimes a tacit or an express understanding insures that the credits secured by the borrowing country will be utilized for purchases in the lending country. Sometimes personal influence will direct the purchases. A citizen of the investing country may become the manager of the private enterprise abroad for the development of which the loan is granted, or in case the loan is made to a government for work in an undeveloped region, the engineer very often will be from the lending country. The manager or the engineer in question will naturally favor with his orders those firms in his home land which he knows or with which he is connected. More decisive than personal influence is the effect of interlocking directorates. British interests becoming directors of a Chinese railroad through a loan to the enterprise may also be directors or stockholders in concerns in England manufacturing steel rails and railway supplies, and they are thus able to require purchases from their establishments.

---

[15] See Angell, Theory of International Prices; and Viner, Canada's Balance of International Indebtedness.

Where the investing interests secure a control of the enterprise to which the loan is granted, the proceeds of the entire investment are very often directed by the investors into purchases which result to their own profit.[16]

Because of the nature of the transactions, it is impossible to say what per cent of foreign loans are granted upon the basis of written agreements or tacit understandings to the effect that the proceeds are to be spent in the lending country. As a case of written agreement, Hurley cites a French banking establishment, Perrier and Company, which had made

. . . a loan of $10,000,000 to the State of Minas Geraes, Brazil, the fund to be loaned out in turn by the State to various municipalities for the perfection of municipal improvements such as tramways and electric lighting plants. The contracts executed between the State as lender and the municipality as borrower stipulated that when other considerations were equal, preference should be accorded by the municipality to French materials, and that in such purchases the municipalities should avail themselves of the mediation of the house of Perrier and Company.[17]

"Tied" Investments in South America.—The following testimony of two American manufacturers before the Federal Trade Commission refers to cases of foreign loans made with stipulations for the expenditure of the proceeds in the lending countries.

In the Argentine, in particular, we have encountered serious difficulty in selling to the railroads, as these are largely controlled by British financial interests. Every possible preference is given to British materials—even though substantial economies may be possible by employing American construction methods and materials. The consulting engineers in London receive a percentage on all materials purchased on designs which they prepare or which may be prepared by the engineers of the railroad and are approved by them.

---

[16] W. S. Culbertson, Commercial Policy in Wartime and After, pp. 311–337; S. Litman, Essentials of International Trade, pp. 56 and ff; H. C. Kidd, Kidd on Foreign Trade, pp. 35 and ff.
[17] Special Agents Series No. 90, p. 47.

Their antagonism toward everything American even led them in one case to adopt a very expensive and antiquated construction, using local materials, rather than approve a design which we submitted and which would have effected a saving of upward of $100,000. Our design was approved and urgently recommended by the chief and assistant engineers in Buenos Aires, but their recommendations were promptly overruled by the consulting engineers and the directors in London.

Another striking case was in connection with a group of large structures. Here again our design which showed a saving of $60,000 to $70,000 was accepted and approved by the engineer in Buenos Aires, but his decision was immediately set aside by the German directors, who advised him that the financing of the project by German capital was conditioned upon German materials being employed throughout.[18]

In several South American countries and in Mexico, English, German and American investments in industrial plants, railroads and public utilities, insure in a large measure orders for machinery and plant equipment being placed with the merchants or manufacturers of the country having the investment. For instance, the investment of Chicago capital in packing houses in Buenos Aires insures the installation of American machinery in these plants, while houses controlled by English capital are equipped with English machinery. In Chile, American mining interests buy American machinery, often at a higher price than similar machinery could be bought for in Europe. Our investments in Mexico, as much as our proximity to that market, is the reason for our having the lion's share of the foreign trade of that country.[19]

Governmental Guaranties.—According to Section I, paragraph 1, of the existing British Trade Facilities Act, bankers may secure the guaranty of the British Government to a foreign loan providing that the proceeds of the loan are to be used for the purchase of articles "manufactured or produced in the United Kingdom." [20] The United States Government has

---

[18] Statement of the representative of a large American company making a steel specialty in Co-operation in American Export Trade, Vol. I, p. 74.

[19] Statement of a manufacturer of power transmission appliances in Co-operation in American Export Trade, Vol. I., p. 75.

[20] Report of the National Foreign Trade Convention, 1924, p. 170.

followed a policy of refusing to guarantee foreign loans made by its citizens and limits its protection of their interests to vigorous diplomatic representations. It has taken no measures to insure the expenditure of such loans in the United States. But as a matter of fact the proceeds of many American loans to foreigners have been spent in this country and the large amount of American lending abroad during the past few years has swelled the volume of our foreign trade. One of the first large foreign loans for construction work after the war was that of $5,000,000 made by the American International Corporation for the construction of a modern sewage disposal system in Uruguay, the work to be done by the Ulen Contracting Company of Chicago and New York. The New York Times in a lengthy article stated that, "Practically every pound of this machinery and material for this construction, not obtainable in Uruguay, is to be sent from this country."

Sentiment Among American Business Men.—Since the United States has become a lending country there has appeared a strong sentiment among American business men interested in foreign trade that foreign loans made by Americans should be used for the purchase of American materials. O. B. Iles, president of the International Machine Tool Company of Indianapolis, speaking at the fourth annual convention of the American Bankers Association for Foreign Trade, remarked to the bankers,

We think there is an opportunity under present conditions for the bankers to be of real constructive service to the manufacturers of machinery and equipment in the United States. When money is furnished to build and equip a railroad, have a thought for the welfare of the manufacturers of railroad equipment and machine tools in the United States. Insert a clause in the contract that this equipment be bought in the United States if possible, and give all manufacturers in the United States a chance at the business. We question the moral, ethical, and economic right of our bankers to furnish the capital to injure our business and to make such loans without a thought for our welfare and indirectly the welfare of our whole business.[21]

The final declaration of the National Foreign Trade Convention of 1926 contained the following statement:

> In the flotation in this market (the United States) of foreign loans, our bankers have opportunity to be of substantial service to American foreign trade. The present situation calls for the exercise of constant care and prudence, lest American capital be devoted to uses detrimental rather than helpful to American enterprise. It is of the utmost importance that our bankers, when negotiating foreign loans, should always have regard to the furtherance of American trade and they should, as far as practicable, provide for the expenditure of the proceeds in this country.[22]

In quitting the subject of foreign investments and foreign trade the following observations are in order. Foreign loans with provisions by written agreement, tacit understanding or other methods to insure the expenditure of the loans in the lending countries certainly have been made on numerous occasions but such loans constitute only a small proportion of the total mass of foreign investments and their number and importance is exaggerated by most writers. But it must be observed that the making of foreign loans by a nation affects its foreign trade whether those loans are "tied" or not; the immediate effect is to increase its exports either to the borrowing country or to other countries, the ultimate effect (when interest payments exceed annual new loans) is to increase its imports. Mention of foreign investments with stipulations for expenditure in the lending country and of the appearance of a sentiment in favor of such "tied" loans on the part of American business interests presents a condition which most economists view with misgivings. However, it cannot be left out of consideration in a study of American foreign trade and foreign banking.

---

[21] *Bankers Magazine,* May, 1925, pp. 802–803.
[22] Report of the National Foreign Trade Convention, 1926, page ix.

Capital-Export and Branch Banks.—Branch banks are characteristically, although not universally, established by capital-exporting countries. As to the rôle played by the branch bank in the foreign investment of capital, it is said to be that of a channel through which a nation's surplus funds may flow into the most productive employments in the relatively undeveloped countries which are always in great need of capital. Only a small part of foreign investments actually do flow through branch banks, it would seem from a comparison of the volume of the foreign investments of the various nations with the scale of business done by their foreign branch banks. It is true, however, that branch banks may render important services in foreign investment. The branch possesses an advantage in that it is right in the foreign country, and, always alert, can advise its parent institution and affiliated investment houses with promptness of contemplated public works, projected business enterprises, and other profitable possibilities for investment. Such advice cannot be expected from a correspondent bank, yet it is only a part of the extensive information service furnished by branch banks to their home office. The branch is in a position to know local conditions thoroughly and can select the better risks, thereby safeguarding the interests of the investors in its home country. It may underwrite local issues of securities, having the home office market them, or it may purchase the issues of local firms gaining in this manner the control of the purchases and sales of these enterprises. In all cases the investment of capital in the branch's territory by home capitalists should mean trade to be financed by the branch. Some branches working in the interest of their parent institutions and of the merchants and investors of their home countries have built up a close harmony of co-operation between banker, foreign trader and investor. While the rôle of foreign branch banks may appear to be exaggerated in the following statement yet it is true that they have been used as a channel for the investment of considerable funds abroad.

The astonishing development of European commerce in the Latin American countries has in a large measure been due to the assistance furnished to the business men of those nations by their bankers. This aid has not alone taken the form of the discounting of drafts covering shipments to Latin America but also the financing of projects of almost every conceivable nature.

Through the branch banks established throughout Latin America, capital was supplied to industrial concerns, railroads, electric light and power plants, irrigation and water power projects, mines, plantations, etc. When the capital for these enterprises was furnished by the European banks, the purchase of materials from their own manufacturers was naturally insisted upon.[23]

Co-operation between Bankers, Foreign Traders, and Investors.—In summary of the preceding pages we may say that it is by co-operation with the merchants and investment houses of their country or, in some cases, by a policy of outright nationalistic favoritism that branch banks have come to be, by far, the most effective among all methods of foreign banking contact for the promotion of a nation's foreign trade.

---

[23] E. B. Filsinger, *op. cit.*, p. 215.

CHAPTER V

SOME ADDITIONAL REASONS FOR THE ESTAB-
LISHMENT OF FOREIGN BRANCH BANKS

Other Advantages of Branch Banks.—The preceding two chapters deal with the rôle of the branch bank in financing and in promoting a nation's foreign trade and explain the principal reasons for the establishment of branch banks abroad. These principal reasons are bound up with the services of branch banks to foreign trade. But there are motives which may enter into the decision of a bank to establish a foreign branch other than those which have to do with facilitating foreign commerce. In most cases these other motives are, alone, not important enough to impel the installation of a foreign branch bank, but in cases where they are present in addition to the reasons for branch bank establishment already studied they make the case for the establishment of a branch all the stronger. They are to be found as contributary reasons in many cases of foreign branch bank installation.

The Securing of Native Business Abroad.—The profitableness of a branch does not depend altogether upon the amount of foreign trade it helps finance. The branch may do more or less local banking business in the foreign center where it is located. It seems generally true that foreign branch banks established in the great nations do not actively compete for the purely local business of the natives. It is a fact, however, that during the war and post-war periods some newly established American branch banks in Europe, in Paris for example, did try for this type of business and by overliberal credit policies incurred the enmity of the native banks. A number of distinctly local accounts were secured due to the disturbed conditions and to the lack of confidence in native banks caused by the war, but as conditions worked back to normal such accounts were for the most part lost.   At present the general policy of American foreign branch banks in the great nations appears to be neither to seek nor to refuse local accounts for natives. The following note on the foreign branches of British banks may be applied with accuracy to the American foreign branch banks.

Deposit accounts in France, Belgium and Spain are largely for British firms operating locally, or for native firms in connection with their British business. The same is true of loans and advances. Deposit accounts for foreigners in the local currency and for local purposes are not refused; nor are they solicited. It is stated that the efficiency of British banking, and the untoward conditions on the Continent have brought much business, but the competition does not seem to have been active enough to create open ill-will among Continental banks.[1]

But when we turn to the so-called great neutral markets, especially Latin America and the Orient, we find branches of foreign banks doing a great deal of purely local banking business. In such countries foreign branch banks work actively to build up a large business with the natives. The following item may serve as an illustration.

What is considered a world record in building up savings accounts has been accomplished by the Cuban and Porto Rican branches of the National City Bank. When plans were originally laid for the contest, it was hoped to reach a total of 12,000 or possibly 15,000 new depositors, but when the final checking-up came, workers rolled up 30,448, with total initial deposits of $4,304,407. This figure compares with $3,259,335 obtained as the result of a contest held in New York in 1923, when 45,226 new accounts were opened.[2]

Support of American Enterprises Abroad.—In addition to receiving accounts from the natives for local purposes in

---

[1] L. R. Robinson, Foreign Credit Facilities in the United Kingdom, p. 91.
[2] *Wall Street Journal,* January 28, 1926.

certain countries, as stated above, the American foreign branch bank may secure accounts from native firms doing business with the United States, and it may also expect to get business from American enterprises and individuals located in its center. In the past there have been but few American concerns located abroad, but the number of such establishments has been growing constantly and today in many of the great foreign cities there are increasing numbers of American business men with whom the American branch bank may enter into relations with profit to itself and to these clients. The lists compiled by the Commercial Intelligence Division in the Department of Commerce of American firms operating in certain foreign countries, although not complete, indicate in some manner the American business penetration in foreign lands. According to these lists there were in round numbers in 1925 about 400 American firms operating in China, 300 in Great Britain, 140 in France, 130 in Japan, 120 in Brazil, 50 in Argentina, 50 in Chile, 50 in India, 30 in Italy, 30 in Spain, 20 in Peru, and 20 in Uruguay. C. D. Snow of the Chamber of Commerce of the United States estimates that there were in 1926 about 4,000 American companies or American citizens (lawyers, doctors, dentists, engineers, etc.) holding memberships in American chambers of commerce abroad. These figures relative to the number of American firms and professional men abroad give some indication of the American enterprises incorporated and private in foreign countries. As to the total number of Americans employed abroad nothing but a mere guess can be made. The Department of State would put it at about 45,000. This figure, of course, does not include the great number of American tourists who go abroad each year, and to which reference will be made later.

The American branch bank abroad offering its services upon as favorable a basis as the foreign institutions may expect to secure much of the banking business of the American firms and their employes and of American professional men due to the natural preference of Americans for bankers of their own nationality. An American business man abroad also argues that business will be attracted from American enterprises because they are accorded more support by American branches than by foreign banks:

> So far as banking operations are concerned, I would like to say this: very often we have found it to our advantage to go to a foreign bank for facilities because it was advantageous to go to them whenever it was a straightforward and easy proposition, but I don't mind adding right here that during the time when we were all up against it in 1920 and '21, the banks that were back of us every minute were the American banks.[3]

Services to Tourists.—American banks situated in certain foreign centers where American tourists pass or stop are in a position to profit by the extension of banking and travel agency services to their countrymen. Every year some hundreds of thousands of Americans tour foreign lands,[4] and most of their banking business abroad is transacted with the foreign establishments of American banking institutions. These people generally prefer to deal with an American branch bank because it knows their needs and takes care of all their difficulties in the way that pleases them.[5] The desire to serve American

---

[3] F. J. Deane, president of the American Chamber of Commerce at Peking, China, speaking before the National Foreign Trade Convention of 1924, page 104 of the Report. It is Laughlin's belief that "So far as Americans are engaged in foreign trade or are located in foreign countries they labor under some disadvantages if they are obliged to do their business through foreign banking institutions. In international trade and in granting loans the trade of any one country is usually favored by the institutions owned by the citizens of that country. Our business men are not so well known that they can obtain loans from foreign banking houses in Buenos Aires or Hongkong as favorably as those who have been long known to their commercial and banking institutions. A young country must fight for its recognition in trade, and it needs the support abroad of its powerful banking institutions." J. L. Laughlin, Banking Progress, p. 274. In the case of the German trading houses taken over in Hongkong at the beginning of the war, however, the records showed that they had leaned more heavily upon English than upon German banks.

[4] In 1925, some 366,605 American citizens returned from abroad and 356,155 left for foreign lands. This does not include those visiting Canada. The amount of money spent by American tourists in foreign contries other than in Canada amounted to $440,000,000 in 1925, according to Trade Information Bulletin No. 399, p. 11. Before the war American tourist expenditures were estimated to be between $150,000,000 and $200,000,000 yearly.

[5] The banks realize this preference and make a point of it in their advertising. A bank having a branch in Paris states in a leaflet distributed in the United States: "When in Paris you are cordially invited to utilize this office and enjoy the advantages of an American bank, employing American methods, in a country where the language and customs are different than at home."

tourists has been a motive for branch bank establishment in a number of foreign centers, and especially in London and Paris. A brochure of the Equitable Trust Company states: "Our offices in London have been established with the following two-fold purpose in view: (a) to assist in financing the ever-growing export and import trade among Great Britain, her colonies and the United States; and (b) to accommodate and serve the ever-increasing number of American visitors to London." In some of the great world centers the amount of business done by the American branch bank for American tourists and for the American concerns and citizens mentioned in the preceding paragraphs account for a considerable part of the business of the branch.

The Branch as an Advertisement.—A firmly established and well equipped branch bank not only advertises our country and advances the prestige of the United States in the foreign land where it is located thereby promoting tendencies towards better commercial relations, but it constitutes a valuable advertisement for the home bank itself. American tourists are much impressed by finding branches of a home bank in the lands they visit thousands of miles from their native country and tend to enter into relations with that bank when they return. The bank also attracts the business of foreigners, and of domestic and foreign correspondent banks because it seems evident to all that an institution able to maintain foreign branches must be an establishment of the first rank. In some of the great cities of the world, notably Paris and London, the advertising value and the prestige accruing to the parent institution from a branch located in these centers is considered to be so important by some banks that it is said they would maintain such branches even at a loss.

Exchange Operations.—Another direct advantage of the branch to the parent institution is to be found in the favorable situation of the branch for large exchange operations. A bank having branches in a number of great financial centers can engage in profitable exchange transactions, shifting funds from one market to another in search of the most advantageous employment and profiting from the differences in exchange without having to share its commissions with a correspondent. In all the world financial centers, the various branches of foreign banks engage in exchange operations which run up into considerable figures.

The Branch as an Investment.—Foreign writers mention as a motive for the establishment of foreign branch banks the good returns on capital invested in branches in capital-poor countries where rates of interest are high. The importance of this motive is suggested by the direction of the foreign branch expansion of the great banks of the world—the movement having been predominantly toward countries with a relative scarcity of capital. Before the war the appeal of the branch bank as an investment exercised more pressure toward the establishment of foreign branches in the case of European banking institutions than in the case of American banks. Opportunities for foreign investment were eagerly sought by Europeans due to the great difference between the return upon such investments and domestic investments, whereas in the United States opportunities presented by investments at home appeared more generally favorable than those offered by foreign lands. One of the effects of the World War, however, was to bring about such a spread between American and foreign rates that considerable amounts of American capital have been attracted abroad, especially since the beginning of 1924.

The Services of Branch Banks.—As an explanation of the reasons for the establishment of foreign branch banks, and of American branch banks in particular, the rôle of branch banks in financing and promoting foreign trade together with some additional advantages possessed by branches has been presented at some length. The advantages possessed by the branch bank in foreign trade: complete responsibility to clients, protection of trade secrets, superior information service, lower cost in financing, better understanding of its nationals, and nationalistic co-operation with merchants and investors of its own country, make it the superior form of banking contact for financing and promoting *important* volumes of trade with foreign markets. The additional reasons for branch bank establishment considered in this chapter: profits from services to natives and American concerns, residents and travelers abroad, and from exchange operations in foreign markets, and the advertising and investment value of foreign branches, have also entered, either singly or collectively, into the decision of banks to install branches abroad.

Such have been the general reasons for the establishment of foreign branch banks. We may now turn to the first period of American foreign branch bank establishment and attempt an explanation of the small foreign expansion of American banks before 1914.

CHAPTER VI

AMERICAN FOREIGN BRANCH BANKS BEFORE 1914

Few Branch Banks Abroad Before 1914.—For a half century prior to the World War the great banks of the world were busy building up systems of foreign branch banks. England, France, Germany, and Holland had by 1914 created important nets of branch banks in foreign countries. As for the United States, the National Monetary Commission, reporting in 1910, declared that the American banking system as a whole was decidedly unsatisfactory, specifying seventeen points in which it was defective, and under point number fifteen we find the statement, "We have no American banking institutions in foreign countries. The organization of such banks is necessary for the development of our foreign trade."

As a matter of fact there were a few American branch banks in the field before 1910. The International Banking Corporation, created for the purpose of establishing foreign branches and engaging in international banking, possessed 16 branches abroad by 1910. This corporation was a specialized institution authorized to engage solely in foreign banking and prohibited from carrying on the regular banking operations in the United States. Only three incorporated American banking establishments doing a regular business in the United States had foreign branches before 1910. These were the Farmers' Loan and Trust Company with two foreign branches, the Trust Company of America with one foreign branch, and the Guaranty Trust Company which had one branch abroad.

By the end of 1913, there were four institutions doing a

domestic business and having foreign branches. The Empire Trust Company had entered the field establishing a branch at London, and the Trust Company of America had liquidated, its London branch being acquired by the Equitable Trust Company which established another branch at Paris. During the year 1913 the Continental Banking and Trust Company of Panama, a foreign banking corporation formed under the laws of West Virginia, was formed. It had established four foreign branches by the end of the year.

Before 1914, therefore, there were only four American domestic banks possessing foreign branches. These banks had a total of six branches. The two American foreign banking corporations had a total of twenty branches. These twenty-six foreign establishments constituted the grand total of the American branch banks abroad at the opening of the decade 1914-1924 which was to witness a striking expansion of American foreign branch banking.

American Foreign Trade

An examination of the overseas expansion on the part of the great banks of the various nations indicates that foreign branch banks are characteristically established by capital-exporting and foreign-trading nations. In the explanation of the expansion and the direction of expansion of a nation's foreign branch banking organization the more important factors to be taken into consideration are: the relative scarcity of capital; the volume, character, and direction of the nation's foreign trade; the banking legislation at home and abroad.

There were but few American branch banks established abroad before 1914 and the direction of the expansion was mainly toward non-European countries. Before 1914 the United States exported but little capital, being in fact a net importer of capital (see American Foreign Investments in Chapter VIII), and the exported capital tended in the direction of the non-European countries where capital was relatively scarce as compared to Europe.

Volume of American Commerce in Foreign Lands.—It has been thought by some that American foreign trade was insignificant before the World War and that Americans were not at all interested in foreign commerce. The increase of American foreign trade has been steady and the growth of interest in foreign markets on the part of American exporters has been continuous. The failure of American banks to establish any large number of foreign branches in the period before the World War was not due simply to the lack of a sufficient *volume* of foreign commerce. It is true that our foreign trade has always been of small importance relative to our internal trade. In the years preceding the World War and today, about 10 per cent may be taken as the proportion of our foreign to our domestic trade.[1] But the unimportance of American foreign trade relative to the internal trade is not of real importance in this study. That which is significant, is the absolute volume of American trade, especially export trade, with foreign countries. The magnitude of our domestic commercial activities has always tended to blind most Americans to the really enormous size of the nation's foreign trade. Even before the war, we were one of the great foreign trading nations of the world. Our total foreign trade rose from $404,774,883 in 1865 to $4,278,892,383 in 1913,—a truly considerable volume in comparison with the foreign trade of the great European nations. The foreign commerce of the United States had increased tenfold in value in the half century preceding the World War and yet it was financed by foreign banks just as completely in 1913 as in 1865. We had taken a place among the great exporting nations of the world and yet while our competitors had developed large nets

---

[1] Various estimates are given in C. M. Pepper, American Foreign Trade, p. 12; Simon Litman, Essentials of International Trade, p. 51; B. M. Anderson, Effects of the War on Money, Credit, and Banking in France and the United States, p. 157; and A. L. Bishop, Outlines of American Foreign Commerce, pp. 75–76.

of branch banks abroad we had no overseas banking organization worthy of the name.

The leading foreign trading nations of the world in the twentieth century are the United Kingdom, the United States, Germany, and France. In 1913, almost one-half of the international exchange of commodities was credited to these four nations, the United Kingdom claiming over one-seventh of the total, Germany over one-ninth, the United States about one-tenth, and France about one-thirteenth. In value of exports, the nations ranked as follows :[2]

United Kingdom	....	$2,556,106,000
Germany	....	2,403,311,000
United States	....	2,329,684,000
France	....	1,326,950,000

In consideration of these figures it is evident that the foreign trade of the United States was far from unimportant in the pre-war period. The United States has, indeed, been one of the three greatest exporting nations of the world for more than a half century,[3] and so the failure of American banks to establish branches abroad before 1914 cannot be said to be due to an insufficient volume of export trade.

Importance of a Large Volume of Trade with Specific Foreign Markets.—Conditions for branch bank establishment are favorable, however, not simply when the total export trade is large but when the amount of trade with a specific foreign market is sizeable. Here it must be observed that most of our trade has been with Europe where there was a relative abundance of capital and where the banking organization was highly developed. Consequently there was not a pressing necessity for American branch bank establishment to handle

[2] Statistical Abstract of the United States, 1914, pp. 688–9. Data for the fiscal year 1913–14. In 1925 the United Kingdom led in total foreign trade with the United States a close second and with Germany and France ranking third and fourth (see page 130). In exports the United States led the world.

[3] Some very interesting tables on the foreign trade of the great nations are to be found in L. and T. Ford, Foreign Trade of the United States, pp. 271–87.

this trade.   Nevertheless the trend of American exports has
been away from Europe during the last fifty years, and toward countries which are "capital-poor" and where the banking systems are not so highly organized.   To further our
foreign trade with such countries branch banks are important.
In these so-called "new countries" branches of European banks
for long exercised great influence, and as our commerce with
these lands grew American branch banks became more and
more desirable.   The percentage of our total exports marketed
in Europe declined from 86.10 in 1880 to 59.9 in 1913.[4]
American exports during this time were increasing at a great
rate, and although the amount of exports to Europe grew,
those destined to non-European countries increased faster.
The movement away from Europe became more and more
evident in the ten years ending in 1914 when American exports
to Europe increased 40 per cent while those to the countries
of North America increased 125 per cent, to South America
148 per cent, and to Asia and Oceania 110 per cent.[5]   Thus
both volume and direction of American exports grew increasingly favorable to branch bank establishment, and yet
but very few branches were opened.

Importance of the Nature of Trade with Foreign Markets.
—In reference to the favorable condition for branch bank
expansion presented by a large and growing trade with markets
having a lack of capital and undeveloped banking organizations, it must be noted that the nature of the commerce with
such markets may or may not constitute an argument for branch
bank establishment.   If the exports of a nation are mainly
foodstuffs and raw materials there is no real necessity for
the establishment of foreign branch banks because these
products virtually sell themselves and do not require the sup-

---

[4] The decline by decades was: 1880, 86.10 per cent; 1890, 79.74 per cent; 1900,
74.60 per cent; 1910, 65.10 per cent.   In 1920 the proportion of our exports sent to
Europe was 54.27 per cent, and in 1925 it was 53 per cent.
[5] B. O. Hough, Practical Exporting, p. 88.

port of a foreign banking organization. Until 1880 raw materials and foodstuffs, mostly cotton and grain, comprised the bulk of American exports, but since that date exports of manufactured articles have increased steadily with a consequent decrease of the former commodities. The percentage of manufacturers in our exports rose from 15 in 1880 to 49 in 1913.[6] In American import trade finished manufactures showed a constant decrease while crude materials for use in manufacturing and manufactures for use in further manufacturing increased.[7] The change in the nature of American exports since 1880 presented a strong argument for the establishment of branch banks in foreign markets.

From this brief mention of the trend of American foreign trade before the world war period it is evident that there was no real necessity for the establishment of American foreign branch banks as late as the last quarter of the nineteenth century. Our exports were mainly to Europe, the volume going to non-European countries being relatively small in each particular case. These exports did not compete with those of the great European nations, and by nature they did not demand banking support for their sale. In these conditions it was obviously good business sense to make use of the European banking organizations.

Change in Volume, Direction and Nature of American Foreign Trade.—But after the beginning of the twentieth century the change became more apparent in the nature and direction of the steadily growing American export trade. The complementary nature of American trade with Europe became less year by year as our country grew steadily into the

---

[6] The increase by decades was: 1880, 15 per cent; 1890, 22 per cent; 1900, 35 per cent; 1910, 45 per cent. In 1925 manufactures and semi-manufactures were 52 per cent of our exports while manufactures, semi-manufactures and manufactured foodstuffs accounted for about 64 per cent of our export trade.

[7] Finished manufactures declined from 33.38 per cent of our total imports in 1875 to 22.51 per cent in 1913; crude materials for use in manufacturing rose from 14.80 per cent to 35.04 per cent; and manufactures for further use in manufacturing increased from 11.89 per cent to 19.27 per cent in the same period. In 1925 finished manufactures represented 18.8 per cent of our total imports, raw materials 40.7 per cent, and semi-manufactures 17.9 per cent.

position of a direct and powerful competitor of the European nations, offering more and more manufactures in the world market. Our exports of manufactured products to non-European lands grew and called for the establishment of American branch banks for their support. As the United States changed from a merchant of raw materials and food-stuffs to a seller of manufactured products a new sales policy was needed, for the sale of manufactures against the competition of the industries of the great manufacturing nations requires a systematic organization of forces for the promotion of export trade. In order to give the exporter a fair chance of marketing his products in face of the competition of his rivals, co-operation between exporter, banker, investor, transportation agent, and government becomes necessary in order to meet similar co-operation on the part of competing nations. Close relations with the undeveloped neutral markets are of primary importance in order to secure additional markets for exported manufactures and a source of supply of raw materials. All this emphasizes the importance of the branch bank. It is only one part of the organization necessary for the active promotion of the trade of a nation competing with the great powers of the world in the foreign field, yet it is one of the most important. In the decade preceding the World War the development in the volume, nature, and direction of our foreign trade provided increasingly favorable conditions for the expansion of American foreign branch banks yet very few foreign branch banks were established by our banking institutions. This leads us to a consideration of certain legal obstacles to the establishment of American foreign banking facilities before 1914.

Legal Restrictions on American Foreign Banking

Legal Restrictions on Foreign Branch Banking.—In the United States an incorporated bank must obtain its charter

either from the federal or from a state government. Until
1914 the national banks, which are those incorporated under
federal laws, were prohibited from establishing branches either
at home or abroad.[8] Only a few important states permitted
banking institutions incorporated under their laws to open
and maintain offices for doing business at other places than
that where the principal establishment was located. Several
of the great American banks, the logical ones to enter upon a
program of foreign expansion, were national banks.

Legal Restrictions on Power to Accept.—In addition to
prohibitions against foreign branch banking American legislation also denied to most incorporated banks the privilege
of accepting drafts or bills of exchange. There was no specific
provision in the national banking legislation authorizing national banks to accept, and the courts held consistently that a
national bank could not accept drafts drawn upon it.[9] The
banking legislation of the states in many cases prohibited
incorporated state banking establishments from accepting or
were silent on this point. These state institutions were first
allowed to accept about 1909 under the laws of some of the
states in which they were domiciled.[10] But the state trust
companies so authorized and the private banks did but a
trifling amount of accepting and no market for American bank
acceptances was built up until after the establishment of the
Federal Reserve System in 1914. The acceptance privilege is
one of the most important powers possessed by banks doing a
foreign business and this subject will be examined at some
length.

---

[8] Section 5190, R.S.: "The usual business of each national banking association
shall be transacted at an office or banking house located in the place specified in its
organization certificate."

[9] Logan County National Bank v. Townsend, 139 U.S., 67, 73, ". . . . a national
bank cannot rightfully exercise any powers except those expressly granted by that Act
(National-Bank Act), or such incidental powers as are necessary to carry on the
business of banking for which it was established." See also Bullard v. Bank, 18 Wall,
589, 593; First National Bank v. National Exchange Bank, 92 U.S., 122, 127; Seligman
v. Charlottesville National Bank, 3 Hughes 647, 21, Fed. Cas., p. 1036.

[10] Report of the Federal Reserve Board, 1919, p. 21.

Lack of a Market for American Bank Acceptances

Because of their superiority over other methods bank acceptances have long been used to finance most of the trade between nations. In the pre-war period, which we are considering in this chapter, London bank acceptances were most generally used to finance international trade, but an appreciable volume of trade was moved by the acceptances of German and other banks. However, there was no market for American bank acceptances. Some of the great American private banks and trust companies had at one time or another done a bit of this type of business, but the American bank acceptance was really, so to speak, unknown.

During the past ten years a market for American bankers acceptances has been built up and acceptances of our banks have been used to finance a large part of our foreign trade. In those transactions where they have been used they were chosen primarily because they promised better facilitation of the transactions and lower costs. Therefore, it is argued that before 1914 the lack of a market for American bank acceptances hindered American foreign trade, especially in importing and in many cases also in exporting. Moreover, it is claimed that American banks were placed in a disadvantageous position in relation to their competitors who suffered no restrictions upon the right to accept. These arguments rest upon the assumption that since financing by American bank acceptances during the past decade has been cheaper in the case of many operations than financing by the acceptances of foreign banks, the same thing would have been true prior to 1914 but for the lack of certain laws, or in other words, that American banking legislation (such as that contained in the provisions of the Federal Reserve Act for the creation of a market for American bank acceptances) alone was necessary for the establishment of dollar exchange and the salvation of American foreign traders and bankers.

As to American banking legislation, it is true that all national banks were prohibited from making bank acceptances and that there were no central banks in the United States to support a market for American bank acceptances, but the great trust companies of New York could accept and there were no legal obstacles to prevent our private banking houses from accepting also. Here it is to be noted that the great accepting banks of London are private banks. Some kind of a market for American bank acceptances, in short, would have been developed before the passage of the Federal Reserve Act had not London acceptances been preferred. They were preferred because of a number of reasons among which may be mentioned the fact that London held the position of a clearing house for international banking, that there was not as much confidence abroad in the stability of our currency as in sterling, and, above all, that discount rates were cheaper in London than in New York and consequently financing through London was cheaper than financing through New York.

In sum, the lack of a market for American bank acceptances in the pre-war period was not solely due to our restrictive banking legislation and the existence of the present market is not simply due to the banking legislation which went into effect in 1914. This is in no way a denial of the great value of the provisions of the Federal Reserve Act for the creation and maintenance of the market for American bank acceptances; in fact, the market would not now be what it is were it not for this legislation. But it is necessary to explain that a currency of unquestioned stability and low discount rates are of fundamental importance for the establishment of a bank acceptance market.

Example of the Use of the Bank Acceptance.—The bank acceptance may be understood by the examination of its use in a particular foreign trade transaction. In financing an import of goods into the United States its manner of use may be something like the following. A New York merchant arranges to import a cargo of coffee from a Brazilian dealer at Santos, and having agreed with him as to terms, goes to his banker. The banker, being informed by the merchant upon all the details of the transaction and being given security or not as his credit may require, issues him a letter of credit. This letter of credit states the terms, time to run, goods to be shipped, insurance, etc., and authorizes the Brazilian shipper to draw on a designated bank which will accept his draft when it is presented.

Financing of American Foreign Trade By English Banks Prior to World War.—It is often preferable today that the importer's own bank or some other American bank should accept the draft, but before 1914 the American importer had his bank arrange with some foreign banking house to accept drafts drawn against his imports. The letter of credit, therefore, always designated some foreign bank as the acceptor,— usually a London bank.

The majority of drafts for American shipments from all over the world were drawn on London, first, owing to the fact that no discount market existed in New York, and secondly, because the names of American drawees were so little known abroad that even where bills were drawn direct they were hard to negotiate.[11]

The New York bank sends a copy of the letter of credit to the London bank which it has designated as acceptor, and gives the importer the original and a second copy. The importer sends the original letter of credit to the Brazilian merchant giving him the authority to draw on the London bank against the shipment of coffee. The exporter then ships the coffee and presents his draft on the London bank, with documents attached, to his home bank. The local bank will discount (buy) the draft readily because of the fact that it will

---

[11] W. F. Spaulding, Foreign Exchange and Foreign Bills, p. 193.

be accepted by a well-known British banking institution. After discounting the draft the native bank sends one duplicate set of documents to the New York bank direct, and the rest with the draft to its branch or correspondent in London, instructing it to present the draft to the London bank for its acceptance.[12] The correspondent does this and then holds the accepted draft till maturity or sells it, crediting the account of the Brazilian bank. All this done, the papers accompanying the draft are sent to the New York bank which receives them usually before the shipment of coffee arrives.

In order to obtain the bill of lading which was sent to the New York bank by the London accepting bank after accepting the draft, and without which he cannot claim the cargo, the American importer makes an agreement with the New York institution under a form known as a "trust receipt." By signing this document he agrees to hold the goods in trust for the bank as its property, and to turn over to it the proceeds of his sales to apply on the acceptance. The bank may at any time cancel this trust agreement and take over the goods or the proceeds of such goods as have been sold wherever they may be found.

Assuming that the accepted bill was drawn to mature in 90 days, the importer has time to sell the shipment, and several days before the maturity of the draft he delivers the necessary funds to the New York bank which draws a demand draft on London and sends it to the London bank in time to enable it to meet its obligations. When this bank pays the acceptance at its maturity, the operation of financing the coffee import is closed.

Advantages of the Bank Acceptance.—The numerous advantages of the bank acceptance are clear from the example

---

[12] The London bank checks the draft and documents with the letter of credit received from New York, and finding them in conformity with the specifications of the letter of credit will accept the draft, and then advise the New York bank in a letter containing the documents.

just given. The shipper is protected in that the goods he sells do not legally leave his possession until a most responsible party, a well-known bank, has bound itself by its acceptance of his draft against the shipment to pay him in full for the value of the goods.   Furthermore, the exporter can readily sell the draft immediately upon drawing it (for it is to be accepted by a bank in good standing), and at a lower rate of discount than that upon a straight draft.[13] If the exporter had sold his cargo cash on delivery (documents against payment) he might have found some trouble in getting the order, and he would have had to wait some time for his money; if he had sold the shipment on open account he would have had to wait a long time for payment,—perhaps he would have had to bring action to secure payment from a customer whose credit standing he had misjudged,—and while waiting for payment it must be remembered that the exporter's own capital is tied up in financing the shipment.

The banks discounting and accepting the draft are protected because the draft is drawn against a bona fide shipment of goods and because the New York bank has bound itself, under the letter of credit, to place the accepting bank in funds to meet the acceptance upon maturity. The New York bank is protected because the acceptance covers a transaction arising from the actual sale of goods and often in addition by security given it by the importer in consideration of the issuance of the letter of credit.   The individual buying the draft in the London market is protected by the high character of the bank acceptance the payment of which is guaranteed by two signatures instead of but one as is the case on single-name paper. Bank acceptances are bought readily by a great class of persons from banks and industrial enterprises to individuals not only because they are so safe but because they are short-term obligations and can be used for employing any idle sums of

---

[13] "The acceptance is the standard form of paper in the world discount market, and both on this account and because of its acknowledged liquidity, universally commands a preferential rate," Federal Reserve Circular of February 8, 1915.

money up to the very day upon which an individual or establishment has payments to meet.

It is because bank acceptances present such a cheap and safe method of financing foreign trade that they are employed for moving most of the trade of the world. American foreign trade before 1914 was financed largely by bankers' acceptances but they were the acceptances of foreign and not of American banks. This condition, as mentioned at the beginning of this discussion, has given rise to a great mass of writing upon the disadvantages to American importers, to American exporters, and to American bankers of the lack of a market for American bank acceptances before the passage of the Federal Reserve Act. A great deal of this writing is rather superficial and most of it presents a serious defect in assuming that before the passage of the Act Americans were suffering disadvantages which necessitated only banking legislation for their removal.

The following quotation, for example, refers to the disadvantages borne by American importers before 1914.

Without bank acceptances we are at a distinct disadvantage in connection with our foreign trade. Our importers, unable to open credit with their banks, as is done abroad, are not in a position to finance their purchases upon as favorable a basis as the importers in other countries.

Without such facilities, the American importer is compelled to finance his purchases in either one of two ways. He may pay for the goods at once by remitting funds direct to the shipper. This, however, ordinarily necessitates the negotiation by the importer of a loan on his promissory note.

If he is not in a condition to secure such an advance, he must shift the burden of providing funds to finance the shipment . . . upon the foreign shipper, who is then in a position to exact terms more favorable to himself through an adjustment of prices. The practice in connection with this method of making payment for foreign purchases is for the shipper to draw his draft on the American importer and turn it over to his banker to forward for collection. Such drafts, drawn as they are on individual importers and not on banks whose standing is well known abroad, must be sent for collection since there is no general market for them. Practically the only way in which a foreign shipper can realize immediately upon bills of this character is to dispose of them to his own banker or get him to make an advance on them.

Either of these two methods of financing our imports is expensive even when the time between the shipment and the receipt of goods is short. When the time is much longer, as in the case of imports from South America and the Far East, the cost is almost prohibitive,—that is, so great that we cannot compete on an even basis with foreign buyers. In fact we might be practically excluded from these markets if a makeshift were not possible. . . .

As to the makeshift: that of getting a London bank to accept,

This method, while workable, is obviously cumbersome, yet it is practically the only one which the American importer can follow in connection with such imports.[14]

According to the quotation above the American importer could provide for the financing of his imports by: (1) borrowing from his bank and paying cash, (2) having the foreign exporter draw a draft upon him, or (3) having a London bank accept for him. As the quotation indicates, the last method was "practically the only one which the American importer" followed. This was a fact, and it was used because it was the cheapest. Did the American importer suffer a serious disadvantage when he financed through London? He was borrowing in the cheapest market in the world—the discount rates in London prior to 1914 were normally lower than in New York. This relation of the discount rates is really the fundamental fact. The American importer was not forced to use London acceptances, for any importer who could provide a London acceptance could have borrowed from a New York bank, if he preferred, so as to pay cash, or he could have had any one of the great New York trust companies or private banks accept for him. If it had been cheaper for the

---

[14] "Bank Acceptances," National Monetary Commission Report, 1910.

American importer to borrow in New York before 1914 the trust companies and the great private banks, like the London private banks, would have built up some kind of an acceptance business before that date. In order to determine whether the American importer was at a disadvantage before 1914 one must answer the question: whether London commissions plus London discount rates plus the prices at which the use of a London acceptance enabled the importer to buy were larger or smaller than discount rates in New York plus the prices the importer would have to pay if he offered only New York funds. To this it may be replied that financing through London was cheaper than through New York and would no doubt have been generally cheaper even if the present legal provisions on American bank acceptances had been in effect. Today, due to the change of the United States from debtor nation to creditor nation and the low rates of discount in New York, it certainly would be disadvantageous to the American importer if American banks were prohibited from accepting and he had to have his imports financed through foreign centers where higher rates prevail.

To continue the quotation under consideration we find that our exporters were felt to be at a disadvantage.

Since bills cannot be drawn on our banks from foreign points against shipments of goods to the United States, there are consequently in such foreign countries very few bills which can be purchased for remittance to the United States in payment for goods which have been brought here. In other words under our present banking system our imports do not create a supply of exchange on New York, for example, which can be sold in foreign countries to those who have payments to make in New York.

This means that our exporters are also, to their great disadvantage, made dependent upon London. It means that when they are shipping goods to South America and to the Orient they cannot, when they are subject to competition, advantageously bill them in dollars. They naturally do not care to value their goods in local currency,— that is, in the money of the country to which the goods are going,—

so their only alternative is to value them in francs, marks, or sterling, preferably the latter. . . .

When we come to bill our goods in sterling, however, it is at once seen that our exporters are obliged to take a risk of exchange which is a serious handicap when competing with British exporters. If in an effort to safeguard themselves against a loss in exchange they calculate on too low a rate for the ultimate conversion of their sterling into dollars their prices become unfavorable compared to those made by British exporters, and they lose the business. If they do not calculate on a sufficiently low rate, they get the business, but lose money on the transaction through a loss in exchange.

As previously stated, the belief that bills could not be drawn on American banks before 1914 was not entirely true for, although national banks were prohibited from accepting, private banks and New York trust companies could accept. The fundamental reason for billing American exports before the World War in sterling and today in dollars has been the relative position of the London and New York discount rates— in each case the market having the lowest rate has been preferred. The American exporter, it appears, has suffered no more real disadvantage than the American importer.

Some writers have held that the lack of a market for American bank acceptances before 1914 not only constituted a hindrance for American exporters and importers but also meant that a large source of profitable business was lost by American banking institutions to the foreign banks which financed our foreign trade. But the profits on discounting bank acceptances are relatively small, and American banks before 1914 generally did about as much business as their reserves permitted. The payment of commissions to English bankers for financing American foreign trade before the World War gave rise to the expression that we were "paying tribute to London." This was rather an exaggeration, to describe payment for having something done for us more cheaply than our discount rates in New York would allow us to do it for ourselves.

Summary

American foreign banking facilities were extremely poor before 1914 and most of the financing of American foreign trade was done by foreign banks. But it may be said that it was in our interest to take advantage of the cheaper services of foreign banking facilities. If American banks were to finance our foreign trade the establishment of a discount market was necessary. Most writers have agreed that the establishment of a discount market required: the granting to national banks of the right to accept, the establishment of foreign branches by American banks, and the creation of central banks of rediscount to support the market. These requirements demanded federal legislation in each case for their satisfactory fulfillment, and such legislation was invaluable for the most effective maintenance of an American bank acceptance market. But there were other requirements not to be overlooked: the creation and maintenance of this market was dependent first of all upon a currency which other countries could trust and upon low discount rates. After 1914 the provisions of the Federal Reserve Act, especially those for the creation of central rediscounting institutions, helped toward both of these ends. But so did the loss of stability on the part of sterling and other European currencies, and the enormous and unexpected increase of our gold reserves after 1914.

In this study the provisions of the Federal Reserve Act permitting the establishment of foreign branch banks by national banks are of most interest. The volume, nature, and direction of our foreign trade offered a plausible explanation of the failure of American banks to establish many branches abroad in the nineteenth century. But these characteristics of our foreign commerce gradually changed in their significance and, after the beginning of the twentieth century, revealed themselves as arguments for foreign branch bank expansion. It is true that until the war the United States

remained a capital-importing nation, nevertheless it is doubtful
if the small number of American branch banks abroad before
1914 can be explained satisfactorily without reference to the
prohibition in the national banking laws against foreign
branch bank establishment by national banks.

CHAPTER VII

THE BANKING REFORMS OF 1914

Provisions for Adequate American Foreign Banking Facilities.—It was fortunate that federal banking legislation was revised in time to permit American banks to take advantage of the opportunity for foreign expansion offered by the growth of our foreign commerce during the war and post-war periods. The Federal Reserve Act made possible the creation of adequate American banking facilities for our foreign trade. It authorized national banks to establish foreign branches, to own or participate in the ownership of special banking corporations for foreign operations, and to accept drafts, and it also provided for assistance in the creation and maintenance of a market for American bank acceptances by its authorization of the federal reserve banks.

The New York banking law had permitted trust companies organized under its provisions to establish foreign branches before the passage of the Federal Reserve Act. But in 1914 the banking legislation of the State of New York was revised, closely following the Federal Reserve Act in its provisions for foreign banking expansion by the great institutions of that state.

Since nearly all the American institutions interested in expanding their foreign banking business and in establishing foreign branches were either national banks or New York corporations, the provisions of the revised New York banking law which relate to foreign operations are included in this chapter on the dispositions of the Federal Reserve Act for foreign banking machinery.

Authorization of Foreign Branch Banking

Dispositions for Large National Banks.—The Federal Reserve Act was passed on December 23, 1913 but was not carried into effect until November, 1914. As amended, the Act contains several provisions on foreign branch banking. The larger national banks, i.e., those having a capital and surplus of $1,000,000 or more, may establish branches in foreign countries or in the dependencies or insular possessions of the United States. Such banks are also permitted to create foreign banking corporations, under federal or state laws, which are empowered to establish foreign branches and to carry on foreign banking operations but may not engage in a regular domestic banking business. Three ways are thus open to a large national bank in expanding abroad by means of branches: it may establish its foreign branches directly, it may join with other banks in forming a foreign banking corporation which will found foreign branch banks, or it may create its own subsidiary bank to establish branches abroad.[1]

Small National Banks and Foreign Expansion.—The smaller national banks were rather overlooked in the matter of provision for foreign branches when the Federal Reserve Act was passed, but by virtue of an amendment made on September 17, 1919 any national bank, whatever the amount of its capital and surplus, was given the right to co-operate with other banks to form a foreign banking corporation or to invest in the stock of such a corporation. It was felt that the

---

[1] Section 25 of the Federal Reserve Act: "Any national banking association possessing a capital and surplus of $1,000,000 or more may file application with the Federal Reserve Board for permission to exercise, upon such conditions and/under such regulations as may be prescribed by the said board, either or both of the following powers:
"First. To establish branches in foreign countries or dependencies or insular possessions of the United States for the furtherance of the foreign commerce of the United States, and to act if required to do so as fiscal agents of the United States.
"Second. To invest an amount not exceeding in the aggregate ten per centum of its paid-in capital stock and surplus in the stock of one or more banks or corporations chartered or incorporated under the laws of the United States or of any State thereof, and principally engaged in international or foreign banking, or banking in a dependency or insular possession of the United States either directly or through the agency, ownership, or control of local institutions in foreign countries, or in such dependencies or insular possessions."

smaller national banks were not strong enough to take upon themselves the establishment of foreign branches, but that there was no reason for denying them the privilege of participating in the ownership of a bank of sufficient strength to enter the foreign field. This amendment was passed late in 1919 with the object of increasing the number of banking institutions then engaged in foreign operations and thereby providing more adequately for the financing of our foreign trade and for the promotion in a more vigorous manner of the post-war exports of the United States.[2] The total amount of money that could be invested by the smaller national banks in foreign banking corporations was limited as in the case of the larger banks in order that the condition of the investing banks might not be impaired should a foreign banking corporation experience difficulties.

Federal Foreign Banking Corporations.—At the time when the Federal Reserve Act empowered national banks to buy stock in foreign banking corporations, there were several states having banking laws which permitted the formation of such corporations by American banks. National banks could participate in creating or owning such state foreign banking corporations, but it was deemed necessary in 1919 to provide for the creation of federal corporations to specialize in foreign banking. The Government was very much interested in maintaining the enormous post-war trade of the nation, and it was thought that the movement toward the creation of foreign banking corporations would be speeded up if they were organ-

---

[2] Section 25 of the Federal Reserve Act: "Until January 1, 1921, any national banking association, without regard to the amount of its capital and surplus, may file application with the Federal Reserve Board for permission, upon such conditions and under such regulations as may be prescribed by said board, to invest an amount not exceeding in the aggregate five per centum of its paid-in capital and surplus in the stock of one or more corporations chartered or incorporated under the laws of the United States of any State thereof and, regardless of its location, principally engaged in such phases of international or foreign financial operations as may be necessary to facilitate the export of goods, wares, or merchandise from the United States or any of its dependencies or insular possessions to any foreign country: *Provided, however,* That in no event shall the total investments authorized by this section by any one national bank exceed ten per centum of its capital and surplus."

ized under federal law, and their establishment urged as a matter of vital national importance. The Federal Reserve Board desired such federal foreign banking corporations because they would be more completely under the control of the Board and more easily guided in a uniform policy of American foreign trade expansion. Consequently the Federal Reserve Act was amended by the Edge Act of December 24, 1919 which provided for the formation of foreign banking corporations under federal law.[3]

These Edge corporations may be formed by five or more natural persons. They must have a capital stock of at least $2,000,000, and a majority of their shares must at all times be held and owned by citizens of the United States or by companies or corporations the controlling interest in which is owned by citizens of the United States. They possess full banking powers, with these exceptions: they cannot establish branches in the United States, nor can they accept deposits in the United States other than those which are incidental to or for the purpose of carrying out their international or foreign business. The Edge corporations, like the similar state organizations, are to engage principally in but one sort of business, namely, foreign banking operations, and for this reason they are designated "foreign banking corporations."[4]   It was intended by limiting them exclusively to foreign operations to relieve our commercial banks from carrying the entire burden of financing our foreign trade.

In connection with federal foreign banking corporations, it should be noted that the Edge Act permits the corporations formed under it to engage in both commercial banking (short-term credits) and investment banking (long-term credits) whereas commercial banks are limited to short-term operations.

---

[3] See pp. 120-122.
[4] Section 25(a) of the Federal Reserve Act: "No corporation organized under this section shall carry on any part of its business in the United States except such as, in the judgement of the Federal Reserve Board, shall be incidental to its international or foreign business."

In practice, however, the Federal Reserve Board has limited Edge corporations to but one kind of business, it being felt that it was unwise to allow any one institution to carry on both long- and short-term operations.

Federal Reserve Bank Branches.—In addition to the foregoing provisions for foreign branch banking, the Federal Reserve Act empowered the federal reserve banks to establish branches both at home and abroad,[5] in order to secure the most efficient functioning of the Federal Reserve System at home, and to support American banking wherever necessary in foreign countries.

The New York State Banking Law.—Most of the American banking institutions which have foreign branches at present are New York corporations. The banking law of this state was revised during 1913–1914 and the new law went into effect on April 16, 1914.[6] The New York banking law differs from the Federal Reserve Act in that it provides not only that New York banking institutions may, if they possess a capital and surplus of $1,000,000, establish branches abroad, but that they may also locate branches within the United States.[7] Since

---

[5] Section 3 of the Act: "The Federal Reserve Board may permit or require any Federal reserve bank to establish branch banks within the Federal reserve district in which it is located or within the district of any Federal reserve bank which may have been suspended."

Section 14(e) of the Act permits federal reserve banks to appoint correspondents and "to establish agencies in such countries wheresoever it may be deemed best for the purpose of purchasing, selling, and collecting bills of exchange, and to buy and sell, with or without its indorsement, through such correspondents or agencies, bills of exchange (or acceptances) arising out of actual commercial transactions which have not more than 90 days to run, exclusive of, days of grace, and which bear the signature of two or more responsible parties, and, with the consent of the Federal Reserve Board, to open and maintain banking accounts for such foreign correspondents or agencies."

[6] The commission created by the law, "L. 1913, ch. 705," enacted May 24, 1913, revised the New York banking law, and the revised law, "L. 1914, ch. 369," which is the present law, became effective on April 16, 1914.

[7] Article 3, paragraph 110 of the law: "Any bank having a combined capital and surplus of one million dollars or over, may with the written approval of the superintendent open and occupy a branch office or branch offices in one or more places located without the State of New York, either in the United States of America or in foreign countries."

". . . . a bank in a city which has a population of more than fifty thousand may open and occupy in such city one or more branch offices for the receipt and payment of deposits and for making loans and discounts to customers of such respective branch offices only . . . ."

the several states prohibit the establishment in their territory of branches by banks not created under their own laws, New York institutions are in reality limited to establishing branches abroad or within the borders of New York State. Within the state only banks in a city of 50,000 population or more may open branches, these branches being limited to the city in which the bank is located.

New York banking establishments may also form, or become owners of, foreign banking corporations organized under the laws of an American state. The provisions in the New York banking law relating to the formation of foreign banking corporations are similar to those embodied in the Edge Act.[8] Five or more natural persons may form a New York foreign banking corporation which must have a capital and surplus of at least $2,000,000. The general powers of the corporation are like those of the federal foreign banking corporations. It may receive deposits without the state of New York, but not within the boundaries of the state. A New York foreign banking corporation's branch "established in a country or province of Asia in which the principal local currency consists of silver coin or bullion," may issue, "notes payable in the local currency to bearer on demand without interest." This power has been made use of by branches of New York and of Connecticut corporations located in the Orient.

Provisions for an American Bank Acceptance Market

The Federal Reserve Act.—By the Federal Reserve Act, national banks were for the first time in our history allowed to accept drafts drawn upon them. These drafts may not have over six months to run and may arise out of the importation or exportation of merchandise, or out of the domestic shipment of goods, or be secured by a warehouse receipt or bill

---

[8] Section 3507 of the General Statutes of Connecticut contains similar dispositions and under it some American foreign banking corporations were organized.

of lading covering readily marketable staples.[9]   Drafts to create dollar exchange may be accepted by American member banks of the Federal Reserve System only when drawn by bankers in certain foreign countries designated by the Federal Reserve Board, and must not have more than 90 days sight to run.

The federal reserve banks were authorized by the Federal Reserve Act to discount paper offered to them by member banks, as well as acceptances having a maturity at the time of discount of not more than three months sight to run,[10] and to buy in the open market, bankers' acceptances and bills of exchange with or without the indorsement of a member bank.[11] These powers of the federal reserve banks together with the power to accept accorded to national banks were granted for the purpose of assuring the creation of a market for American bank acceptances.   By these open market operations, the federal reserve banks are enabled to make their discount rates effective and to employ their surplus funds profitably when few member banks are calling for rediscounts.

Acceptances by New York State Banking Establishments. —The provisions in the New York banking law on acceptances were modeled after the acceptance dispositions of the Federal Reserve Act, and are more liberal in regard to the time drafts for acceptance may have to run.   A bank or trust company incorporated under the laws of the State of New York has the right:

---

[9] Section 13 of the Federal Reserve Act: "Any member bank may accept drafts or bills of exchange drawn upon it having not more than six months sight to run, exclusive of days of grace, which grow out of transactions involving the importation or exportation of goods; or which grow out of transactions involving the domestic shipment of goods provided shipping documents conveying or securing title are attached at the time of acceptance; or which are secured at the time of acceptance by a warehouse receipt or other such document conveying or securing title covering readily marketable staples."

[10] Section 13 of the Act.

[11] Section 14 of the Act: "Any Federal reserve bank may, under rules and regulations prescribed by the Federal Reserve Board, purchase and sell in the open market, at home or abroad, either from or to domestic or foreign banks, firms, corporations, or individuals, cable transfers and bankers' acceptances and bills of exchange of the kinds and maturities by this Act made eligible for rediscount, with or without the indorsement of a member bank."

To accept for payment at a future date, drafts drawn upon it by its customers and to issue letters of credit authorizing the holders thereof to draw drafts upon it or its correspondents at sight or on time not exceeding one year,[12]

whereas the national banks cannot accept drafts having more than six months to run.

Summary

Banking Legislation and American Foreign Banking Facilities.—The American incorporated banks which have established branches abroad have been created under federal legislation or under the banking legislation of the states of New York and Connecticut.[13] The Connecticut banking law is similar to the New York legislation in its provisions for foreign banking. The provisions for foreign branch banking and accepting contained in the federal, New York and Connecticut banking laws are of great importance.[14] They permit the great national and state banks to establish foreign branches without any legal hindrance. The passage of the Federal Reserve Act was especially important for American foreign branch banking, for although some state institutions could establish branches abroad and could accept before 1914, the entire group of national banks was prohibited from the exercise of both of these powers. Moreover, even though private banks and some state corporations were able to accept before the enactment of the federal reserve law, some sort of central institution to rediscount and to support the market was desirable.

---

[12] New York Banking Law: Article 3, paragraph 106.

[13] The Continental Banking and Trust Company (West Virginia), 1913–1922 was the only exception.

[14] "Without the aid of the (American) branch banks in Colombia and the system of discounts at home it would be impossible for the exporters to finance the entire volume of trade now on hand, and the branch banks are also helping the local merchants with additional commercial loans and information, and are materially assisting them in extending their business—all these activities being of direct benefit to American foreign trade." Special Agents Series No. 206, 1921, p. 334.

CHAPTER VIII

AMERICAN FOREIGN TRADE SINCE 1914

The Increase in American Foreign Trade

America's Great War and Post-War Trade.—The rapidly growing foreign trade of the United States had raised our nation by 1913 to a firm position among the greatest foreign trading countries of the world, but for seven years after this date our trade no longer simply grew in value; it leaped into amazing figures. From a total of $4,278,892,383 in 1913 the foreign commerce of the United States rose to $13,508,-157,959 in 1920. Due to the abnormal situation growing out of the World War the European nations found themselves unable to provide for their own wants to say nothing of continuing to supply their customers in the great neutral markets. European and non-European nations turned to this country to meet their needs and the United States became the great source of supply for the world.

American Foreign Banking Expansion.—It was during these periods of war and post-war boom that the great American foreign banking expansion took place, branches being established all over the world. The great trade in munitions of war and supplies with Europe together with the necessity of providing banking support for the American military and naval forces in the Eastern Hemisphere led to the establishment of numerous American branch banks in Europe. The increase of American banks in France between 1913 and 1920 was especially noticeable. Not only was most of the American expeditionary force stationed in France but the growth of Franco-

American trade was remarkable in the war and post-war periods, increasing from 1,317,365,000 francs in 1913 to 13,122,612,000 francs in 1920.

After the world crisis of 1920 the value of American foreign trade fell through 1921 to a low of $6,944,524,307 for 1922 and then rose steadily to a total of $9,137,110,280 for the year 1925.[1] The years 1920 to 1925 marked the period of contraction of American foreign banking. The movement of withdrawal of foreign branch banks ended by 1925 and since that year the tendency has been toward slow expansion.

Changes in Nature and Direction of American Foreign Trade.—The changes in the nature and direction of American foreign trade, apparent before the World War (Chapter VI), have continued. In 1925 finished manufactures, semi-finished manufactures and manufactured foodstuffs constituted almost 64 per cent of our total export trade while raw materials and semi-finished manufactures accounted for 58½ per cent of our total imports. Non-European countries took 39.6 per cent of our exports in 1913 and 47 per cent in 1925. They furnished 51.8 per cent of our total imports in 1913 and 70.7 per cent in 1925. This slow change in the direction of American foreign trade away from Europe and toward the relatively less developed countries is of importance in this study because it is in these latter markets that the greatest opportunities for American branch bank expansion are to be found. The war gave Americans an excellent opportunity to secure a foothold in these neutral markets, and, regardless of the loss of a certain amount of business experienced as the European nations have been returning to compete more seriously with us, the preservation of a large American business with these markets may be counted on. In view of the great importance that the posses-

---

[1] The various figures upon the value of American foreign trade from 1913 to 1925, although they do not represent corresponding changes in the volume of our commerce, are those which are of importance in the study of the expansion and contraction of the business of banking. The volume of American export trade in 1925 was 31 per cent greater than it was in 1913.

sion of foreign markets is to have upon the future prosperity of the United States the great American trade with non-European countries during the last ten years was fortunate. This trade advertised American products to foreigners and gave them the opportunity of comparing our goods with those of other countries. Most important of all it broke down to an appreciable extent the old custom in non-European countries of looking to the continent for everything, and built up new connections with the United States.[2]

Co-operation in American Export Trade

Growth of Interest in American Foreign Trade.—The World War not only speeded up the changes taking place in the volume, nature, and direction of American foreign commerce but it also had another interesting effect in developing co-operative effort for the active promotion of American export trade; co-operation by American interests in foreign operations and co-operation by the American Government with these interests.

From 1914 to 1917 American exports were stimulated by the increased demands of foreign nations due to the war, and from the entry of the United States until the armistice, production and exportation were made matters of national importance for the winning of the war. When the conflict ended the productive forces of the United States were keyed up to such a pitch that a great volume of export trade was necessary if

---

[2] The following news item from the *Wall Street Journal* of November 19, 1925, is interesting in this connection.

"WINNIPEG—To develop Canada's foreign trade the Economic Conference decided to form a permanent association, to meet annually, cooperating with the Trade and Commerce Departments of the Federal Government. Delegates from the west coast recited that in the Orient American manufactured products were everywhere supplanting the British made, and that United States firms readily put up containers similar to those that had established English factory products through Japan and China. In South America, these Vancouver delegates asserted, they had found everywhere encroachments of United States commercial travelers on domain that had for a quarter of a century been served through British agencies. Cameras, farm machinery, sewing machines, canned goods and musical instruments were cited particularly as articles in which Yankee ingenuity was penetrating Oriental and South American markets where British goods previously held first place on the shelves of alien merchants of those countries."

American industries were to continue running upon the level attained. The great trade expected did materialize but was of short duration, receiving a decisive check at the end of 1920. For seven years, however, foreign trade had received such an emphasis in the United States as it had never before enjoyed, and during this time Americans had been brought to think seriously upon successful foreign trade methods and to realize the necessity of organized, co-operative effort as a basis for American foreign trade expansion.

The years immediately preceding the war were marked with numerous conventions and conferences in the United States which testified to a growing and lively interest in this country in the expansion of foreign trade.[3] Organizations having for object the facilitation and promotion of American foreign commerce were formed by business men. The Philadelphia Commercial Museum, one of the largest in the world, had been founded as early as 1894, and the National Association of Manufacturers was created in 1895. But in the decade preceding the outbreak of the World War the tendency toward association for foreign trade advancement was marked. The American Exporters and Importers Association was formed in 1907, the American Manufacturers Export Association in 1911, and the Chamber of Commerce of the United States in 1912. The creation of the Bureau of Foreign and Domestic Commerce with its commercial attachés and special trade commissioners in 1912 was a step of real significance taken on the part of the Government. The establishment of the National Foreign Trade Council by American business men in May, 1914 to "endeavor to co-ordinate the foreign trade activities of the nation" was an event of prime importance. The organization has held a convention every year since and has become increasingly important.

---

[3] For example, the Pan-American Commercial Conference at Washington, February, 1911; the Clark University Conference, May, 1913; the First National Foreign Trade Convention at Washington, May, 1914; the Latin American Trade Conference at Washington, September, 1914.

Co-operation for Foreign Trade by Shipping, Banking and Investment Interests of other Nations.—A report on "Co-operation in American Export Trade" was made by the Federal Trade Commission in 1916 as a result of an investigation of the national organizations in foreign countries for the promotion of foreign trade. The report stressed shipping, foreign banking and foreign investment in the foreign trade expansion of our competitors.

Recognizing the vital influence of transportation facilities, foreign nations have built up their ocean shipping, have granted low export railway rates, and have combined their land and ocean transportation facilities to give their shippers ready entrance into their overseas markets. The United States on the contrary has neglected its merchant marine until it is dependent upon its commercial rivals to deliver its goods. In consequence the transportation of its products is now largely controlled by powerful international combinations of foreign shipowners who discriminate against American shippers.

Realizing the necessity of banking and credit facilities to finance their transactions, foreign nations have not only established connections with banking houses in every land, but have established banks of their own in all parts of the world. Banks with their main offices in London, Berlin, Paris, Rome and Vienna operate hundreds of branches and agencies in South America, the Orient, Australasia, the Levant, all around the coast of Africa, and far within the remote interior. They give the foreign exporter information, extend credit, finance his transactions, and constantly strive to increase the foreign business of the mother country. The few foreign branches of American banks have but recently been established, and in most markets our exporters must depend on foreign bankers.

Though now increasing, American investments abroad are comparatively small. British, German, French and other foreign traders, on the other hand, enjoy a peculiar advantage from the billions of dollars of investments made by their fellow nationals in foreign lands, frequently on the express condition that supplies and equipment should be purchased in the country furnishing the funds. British and German investments in South American railroads and public utilities, French investments in Turkey, and Japanese investments in China and Manchuria are typical examples. In consequence, time and again American manufacturers have found it impossible to sell their products abroad because the prospective customer was forced to purchase from or through interested investors.[4]

In the same year, 1916, the Federal Trade Commission in its annual report called attention to the fact that in other great nations combinations or trusts among industrialists and merchants for the purpose of exploiting foreign markets had been for a long time not only permitted but encouraged by the governments. Doubt and fear as to legal restrictions had prevented Americans interested in exporting from forming combinations for export trade, and the Federal Trade Commission requested that "declaratory and permissive legislation be enacted by Congress to make it clear that such organizations are lawful." [5]

During the last ten years Americans have made some progress along these lines of shipping, foreign banking, foreign investment, and combination for export trade.

American Shipping.—The creation of the United States Shipping Board and the Emergency Fleet Corporation and the passage of the Merchant Marine Act of 1920 were steps taken by the Government in an endeavor to meet the shipping emergency due to the war and to provide ultimately for a privately owned and operated American merchant marine adequate to the needs of national defense and sufficient to carry the greater part of our foreign commerce. In 1914 when the war broke out we had some 1,066,000 tons of shipping registered for foreign trade and on January 1, 1926 the total tonnage was 10,997,628 represented by 2,278 vessels. One hundred and ninety of these ships with a total tonnage of 1,227,821 were privately or government owned passenger ships. The other 2,088 vessels with a total tonnage of 9,769,-807 were freight carriers (general cargo boats and tankers)

---

[4] Pages 3–8 of the Report. The report has been severely criticized by some economists as exaggerating foreign discriminations against Americans.
[5] Report of the Federal Trade Commission, 1916, p. 34.

and a little over half of this tonnage was in private hands. The shipping emergency calling for vessels to transport our troops and carry goods during the war was met but whether the United States is to have a privately owned and operated merchant marine carrying the greater part of its foreign trade remains to be seen.   Here it must be noted that many of the 2,088 American ships classed as carrying foreign trade are simply in the coastwise service, commerce with the West Indies, and nearby foreign service.   It is estimated that on January 1, 1926 there were only 491 American ships having a total tonnage of 2,669,657 engaged in actual foreign service, and of these only 121 general cargo boats and 103 tankers with a total tonnage of 1,109,381 were privately owned.[6]   American vessels carried 10 per cent of our total foreign trade in 1913 and 43 per cent in 1920.   In 1925, 30 per cent of our imports and 27 per cent of our exports were carried in ships flying the American flag.   Up to the present only a small amount of progress has been made toward a privately owned and operated merchant marine which will carry the greater part of our foreign commerce.   The government-owned ships are being operated at a loss and it is the intent of Congress to dispose of the vessels to private operators.   By June 30, 1926 the United States Shipping Board and the Emergency Fleet Corporation had cost the American people over $3,500,000,000, the appropriations for the last fiscal year being $24,330,000.   This is not to be regarded as a "loss" but as a proper war expense and of course does not mean that a privately owned American merchant marine of importance is impossible.   What may be accomplished in the way of transferring our government-owned ships to private hands and what success may be met with by American ship-owners, with or without government aid, in building up a merchant marine are questions which await an answer.

---

[6] Ernest Greenwood, *Industrial Digest*, April, 1926.

American Foreign Investments.—The progress made by Americans in foreign banking expansion (discussed in the following chapter), in foreign investment, and in combining for export trade during the past decade has been appreciable. Before the World War the United States was the world's greatest debtor nation. Against a total of about two billion dollars of American funds invested abroad, foreigners possessed investments in the United States to the extent of more than six billion dollars. The war changed this country into a great creditor nation. Our foreign customers who bought such enormous amounts of goods from us during the period 1914 to 1920 were not able to pay for them in gold, merchandise, or services. In order to make purchases of war materials and supplies from the United States, foreign nations surrendered the greater part of their investments in this country and borrowed huge sums from the United States Government and from American individuals and institutions. During the war period, the greatest part of the debts of foreigners to the United States on account of purchases from this country was settled about as follows:[7]

1. Export of gold to the United States................. $1,029,000,000
2. American securities sold back to the United States by
   foreigners 2,000,000,000
3. Foreign securities (railroads, industrials, municipals, etc.)
   sold to Americans 1,520,000,000
4. Loans by the United States Government to Allied and Associated Powers 7,319,500,000

Long-term credits granted by the United States Government played the major rôle in settling the debts of foreigners to us during the war period. But the total of such loans to foreign powers had been limited to $10,000,000, and over two billions having been granted after the armistice in addition to the large former advances, there remained on October 31, 1919

---

[7] T. H. Boggs, International Trade Balance in Theory and Practice, p. 70. See also B. M. Anderson, Jr., Effects of the War on Money, Credit and Banking in France and in the United States, p. 158, and Review of Economic Statistics, April, 1919, p. 246.

an unexpended balance of only $593,628,111.45.[8]   By this
time the amount of American securities sold back to Americans had reached four or five billion dollars [9] which meant
that practically all of the available American securities held
abroad had been surrendered, and consequently this source
of securing credits for settling debts due Americans was
closed. Thus, in 1919, when foreigners were desirous of making great purchases of reconstruction materials and other
goods from the United States, only one important means of
financing these purchases appeared open: long-term credits
from American individuals and institutions to foreigners. The foreign demand for American exports was great
and the Government was interested in supporting the large
American export trade. Consequently Congress passed the
Edge Act on December 24, 1919 to facilitate the extension
of long-term credits to foreigners through investment trusts.
The act authorized national banks to form combinations for
the purpose of foreign banking or foreign financial operations.[10]   Although corporations might be formed under the
Edge Act to engage in either short- or long-term operations, the desire for institutions which would make possible
the extension of long-time credits was the principal motive
for the law.

The Edge Corporations.—The Edge corporations for foreign financial operations were to make long-term credits available to foreigners in the following manner. The foreign importer would furnish the corporation long-time obligations (industrials, railroads, municipals, etc.), or give a mortgage on
his plant, as collateral to get raw materials or machinery from
America. The corporation using these securities as a reserve
would issue its own debentures for sale to Americans. The

---

[8] Report of the Secretary of the Treasury, 1919.
[9] Report of the Comptroller of the Currency, 1919, p. 10.
[10] See pp. 107–108.

proceeds of the sale would make possible the prompt payment of the American exporter and the foreign importer would have plenty of time in which to settle his debt to the corporation.

The principle of the Edge corporation was applied by a Delaware concern, the "American Foreign Securities Company," during the war, and made possible the purchase of $100,000,000 of material from American manufacturers by the French Government.[11] Incorporated July 14, 1916 with a capital of $10,000,000, the corporation made a contract with the French Government four days later for a loan of $100,-000,000 to run from August 1, 1916 to July 31, 1919. The French Government gave its note and $120,000,000 of securities including the obligations of many foreign governments and of American and Canadian corporations. The corporation using these obligations as security issued its own three-year 5 per cent gold notes, dated August 1, 1916 to August 1, 1919, and sold them in July, 1916. They were paid in full at maturity.

Americans had never been very active in purchasing foreign securities and it was thought that by the employment of the investment trust idea of the Edge corporation American long-term credits could be more easily obtained for foreigners than by the direct sale of foreign securities in the United States. It appeared certain that American investors would readily buy the debentures of an Edge corporation for the corporation would be American and the debentures would be backed by a well-selected and diversified list of foreign securities. No Edge corporations, however, were formed in time to help finance the post-war boom. The risks presented by the uncertain political and economic situation abroad, the doubtfulness of the advisability of extending more credits when American banks and manufacturers were loaded with foreign accounts which were proving hard or impossible to collect, and the pressure for credit at home were obstacles to the success

---

[11] H. G. Moulton, *op. cit.*, pp. 266–7.

of the corporations. The first Edge Corporation, the First Federal Foreign Banking Association, New York, was created in 1920 with a capital of $2,100,000 and the second, the Federal International Banking Company, New Orleans, began business in 1921 with a capital of $7,000,000. These two corporations were of the acceptance type and were soon liquidated. A third Edge corporation, debenture type, to have a capitalization of $100,000,000 was proposed in 1920 at the convention of the American Bankers Association in Chicago. Its articles of association and its organization certificate were approved by the Federal Reserve Board on January 28, 1921 and some stock was sold but the project fell through and in 1922 the undertaking was abandoned.

Finally, an Edge corporation, debenture type, the First Federal Foreign Investment Trust was authorized on May 24, 1926 to commence business with a capital of $2,000,000. The corporation is located in New York and was formed to provide for municipalities, land banks, public utilities, and industrial organizations for periods exceeding the usual time limits as fixed by commercial banking practice and in amounts too small for public offerings. Several investment trusts to deal in foreign securities have been formed under state laws.[12] Of these the International Securities Trust of America formed in 1921 with a capital of $9,000,000 is the most important.

The War-Finance Corporation.—Before leaving this subject of the Government's efforts to provide for the creation of institutions to aid American export trade with long-term credits the War-Finance Corporation must be noticed. This corporation was created on April 5, 1918 to facilitate the export of American agricultural and industrial products necessary for the prosecution of the war and for reconstruction purposes by the granting of long-term credits to Americans.

---

[12] L. R. Robinson, Investment Trust Organization and Management, 1926. See also L. M. Speaker, Investment Trust.

The corporation had the power to make advances not exceeding five years to American exporters unable to obtain funds
upon reasonable terms through banking channels and to banks,
live stock loan companies, and co-operative marketing associations. The corporation was capitalized at $500,000,000 and
the aggregate of its advances at any one time was limited to
$1,000,000,000. On January 1, 1925 the corporation entered
into liquidation as provided for by law. It had made advances, since its creation in 1918, aggregating $689,715,000,—
$306,771,000 under its war powers, $85,001,000 for export
purposes, and $297,943,000 for agricultural and live stock
purposes.

Rise of the United States as a Creditor Nation.—It will
be recalled (page 119) that the long-term loans to foreigners
by which the great American export trade between 1914 and
the end of 1918 was mainly financed were made for the most
part by the American Government. Foreign securities sold
to Americans during this period amounted to only a little over
$1,500,000,000. After the armistice the remainder of the
credits granted to foreign nations by the United States was
soon used up and the burden of financing our export trade fell
mainly on the commercial banks since American individuals
and institutions did not step forth to take the place of our
Government in providing long-term credits for foreign bor--
rowers. In 1919 the total foreign loans made by Americans
amounted to $670,000,000 and averaged only $624,500,000
per year for the succeeding four years. It was not until 1924
that the outflow of American funds for investment abroad
assumed extraordinary proportions. During the calendar year
1924 foreign loans made by Americans totaled $1,243,000,000
and during 1925 they amounted to $1,326,900,000.[13]   On

---

[13] See *Bankers Magazine*, 1925, p. 804, and *Commercial and Financial Chronicle*,
February 6, 1926, p. 694. The yearly volume of foreign loans made by Americans was:

1919........$670,000,000		1923........$ 390,000,000
1920........ 634,000,000		1924........ 1,243,000,000
1921........ 628,000,000		1925........ 1,326,900,000
1922........ 846,000,000		

January 1, 1926 the total amount of American foreign investments, exclusive of some twelve billion dollars owed to the
Government of the United States by foreign governments,
was nearly ten and one-half billion dollars as compared with
between two and three billion dollars in 1913. According to
the Department of Commerce, the total foreign investments of
Americans amounted to $10,405,000,000 at the end of the
calendar year 1925.[14] This was distributed as follows:

	Government Guaranteed Obligations	Industrial Securities and Direct Investments	Total
Latin America	$ 910,000,000	$3,300,000,000	$ 4,210,000,000
Canada and Newfoundland.	1,175,000,000	1,650,000,000	2,825,000,000
Europe	1,825,000,000	675,000,000	2,500,000,000
Asia, Australia, Africa, and rest of the world........	520,000,000	350,000,000	870,000,000
	$4,430,000,000	$5,975,000,000	$10,405,000,000

United States Investments in Latin America.—Mention
must be made of the fact that the first column contains a considerable amount that really belongs in the industrial column,
i.e., many loans guaranteed by foreign governments but nevertheless devoted to industrial purposes. It will be noted that
by far the largest part of the investments, over $4,000,000,000,
was made in Latin America. This should appear promising
to those who have wished to see American foreign trade and
foreign banking expansion in the South American countries.
As Dr. H. P. Willis stated in 1917:

In South America, for example, there will be little development of
American trade unless the United States is willing to supply the capital for the financing of Brazilian enterprises on a long term basis.
. . . There is no reason why international banking should be developed
by Americans much more largely than at present pending the time

---

[14] Trade Information Bulletin No. 399. During the first half of 1926 $578,853,500
of foreign securities were offered in the United States. $149,195,300 of these were for
refunding purposes, leaving $429,658,200 as new foreign loans for the first six months
of 1926. Latin America took $176,746,000, Canada $180,715,000, Europe $211,602,500
(of this amount Germany alone took $159,720,500), and $9,790,000 went to the Far East.
Commerce Reports, July 19, 1926, pp. 143–6.

when the United States is ready to furnish the capital that is needed by the business men and producers in the countries with which trade is being built up.[15]

Capital-Hungry World.—The margin between domestic and foreign rates on loans and the constantly bettering state of the world economic organization since 1924 have kept up the great flow of American funds abroad, and the movement promises to continue for some time for the world is capital-hungry and America alone seems capable of rendering aid in important proportions.[16]   The immediate effect of the investments has been to increase American export trade.   When, in a few years, payments of interest to the United States by foreigners exceed the annual foreign investments of Americans they will tend to keep up American foreign commerce through an increase in the imports item.   Our foreign investments are thus stimulating our foreign trade and will contribute to its future support.

Combinations for American Export Trade.—The Webb-Pomerene law, legalizing combinations among American exporters, represented an effort on the part of the United States Government to favor the expansion of American export trade by putting Americans on a more equal basis in competition with the exporters of other nations.   Foreign nations have permitted and encouraged their industrialists and merchants to form trusts for export trade.   This has been especially true of Germany, Italy, Switzerland, Holland, Sweden, Belgium, and Japan and it was believed that, if American exporters were to meet successfully the competition of the export combinations

---

[15] H. P. Willis, American Banking, pp. 81 and 83.   At this time, 1917, Filsinger (*op. cit.*, p. 6) estimated that the United States had only $1,725,450,000 invested in all Latin America.

[16] For example, J. P. Morgan and Company of New York took $75,000,000 of the $100,000,000 issue of Australian bonds in 1925.   The British financiers, who would have normally handled the issue, were not in a position to absorb such an amount at the time.   During the ten years ending December 31, 1924, foreign loans, exclusive of government war loans, floated in the United States aggregated $8,711,950,064 compared with $3,033,003,630 floated in London during this period.

of these countries, combinations among American exporters had to be permitted. Not knowing whether American anti-trust laws would apply to trusts for export business and fear-ing possible prosecution under these laws, Americans inter-ested in foreign trade had not created export trusts and it was claimed that the foreign trade of our manufacturers and mer-chants, particularly the smaller concerns, suffered in conse-quence.

The Guaranty Trust Company of New York, in an in-teresting brochure on the subject, stated:

> In various manufacturing industries, higher manufacturing cost and comparative inexperience in export trade make it extremely diffi-cult at best for Americans to compete with foreigners for trade abroad. Therefore, meeting severe competition from powerful com-binations, and through dependence on foreign cable and telegraph companies, foreign banks and ships, forced to risk exposure of the secrets of their overseas business to their foreign competitors, Ameri-can manufacturers, and especially the smaller producers, have been at a decisive disadvantage in export trade.[17]

The Export Trade Act.—The Export Trade Act (Webb-Pomerene Law) approved April 10, 1918, authorizing combi-nations of American exporters, was the reply to the request of the Federal Trade Commission, made some two years previous, that "declaratory and permissive legislation be enacted by Con-gress to make it clear that such organizations are lawful." The Act amended sections 1, 2, and 3 of the Sherman Anti-Trust Act of July 2, 1890, and section 7 of the Clayton Act of October 15, 1914 to the extent that it authorized the for-mation of combinations engaged solely in export trade. It also amended the Federal Trade Commission Act of September 26, 1914 by extending the prohibition against unfair methods of competition and the remedies for enforcing this prohibition

---

[17] Combining for Foreign Trade, 1920. The importance of the amount of trade handled by the export combinations of foreign countries in relation to the total amount of export trade of these countries is usually exaggerated. But if it be argued, there-fore, that there was no great necessity for legislation permitting combinations of American exporters, it cannot be denied that hundreds of American firms have found this legislation to be of great value.

to "unfair methods of competition used in export trade against competitors engaged in export trade even though the acts constituting such unfair methods are done without the territorial jurisdiction of the United States." [18]

Trusts or combinations for export trade are legalized by the Act, but these trusts may not restrain trade within the United States nor enhance or depress prices in this country of the commodities of the class exported by them. They are associations for export business only, i.e., "for the sole purpose of engaging in trade or commerce only in goods, wares, or merchandise exported or in the course of being exported from the United States or any territory thereof to any foreign nation," and shall not "engage in the production, manufacture, or selling for consumption or for resale, within the United States or any territory thereof, of such goods, wares, or merchandise, or any act in the course of such production, manufacture, or selling for consumption or for resale." [19]

Every trust or association engaged solely in export trade must register with the Federal Trade Commission within 30 days after formation and must file certain statements with the commission on January 1st of each year.[20] By June 30, 1918, 48 associations had filed reports; one year later 92 associations representing 840 member concerns filed reports; during the year ending June 30, 1920, 43 associations comprising 732 concerns filed statements, and on October 1st, 1926, 51 associations representing more than 500 producers throughout the United States and exporting raw materials and manufactures to all parts of the world were operating under the Export Trade Act.

Advantages of Combination.—Advantages obtained by combining for foreign trade under the Export Trade Act are

---

[18] Annual Report of the Federal Trade Commission for 1920, p. 65.
[19] The Export Trade Act.
[20] Statements giving location of place of business, names and addresses of all officers, stockholders or members, copy of certificate of incorporation and by-law, etc.

stated in the following reports made to the Federal Trade Commission by various American export associations.[21]

An association exporting food products to Europe and other parts of the world states:

The advantages gained by the industry in its operations through this association become increasingly evident the more it is operated. The intelligent distribution of stocks throughout the world, the centralization of the statistical and other information so necessary for the extension of trade, and the ability to standardize the quality of the American products to an increasingly higher level are all amply demonstrated by the encouraging increase in business done during the last year.

The competition arising abroad from associations, trade combinations, etc., is and probably always will be a serious factor, although its importance as an obstacle to the expansion of American trade abroad in this industry is discounted to some extent by the advantages gained through our manufacturers being able to operate export associations.

Another association exporting manufactured goods through its agencies in Brazil, Argentina, Uruguay, Chile, Peru, Cuba, Mexico, and the Far East states:

Export selling through an association is decidedly advantageous; it presents a united front to foreign competition, concentrates and simplifies the problem of sales, eliminates unnecessary competition amongst manufacturers, insures an equitable distribution of export business, stabilizes prices in foreign markets, restrains speculation, and generally builds up the prestige of American manufacturers abroad through the intelligent and constructive creation of a uniform sales policy based on cooperation.

An association exporting raw materials to Europe reports that:

By operating under the association, members are enabled to maintain an organization for exploiting foreign markets and gathering data for the general benefit of all which would be too costly for any one member to maintain alone. The data that can be gathered by a

---

[21] Report of the Federal Trade Commission, 1925, pp. 98–99.

single, large, well-directed organization is unquestionably more accurate and reliable than that which could be gathered by a number of smaller organizations working against each other. Similarly, the exploitation of foreign markets can be better handled by a large, single, and well-directed organization than by a number of smaller organizations all working against each other. Concentration of effort, standardization of grades, lower selling costs, are a benefit not only to the American exporter but also to the foreign consumer as well and are important factors in the endeavor to increase export sales.

A number of associations report that their members would be unable to export if it were not for their organization under the act. One states that:

If each individual were attempting to get his share of the business, the cost would be out of all proportion to the possible profit.

An association exporting lumber reports:

The export trade act is decidedly advantageous to most manufacturers of lumber, because they individually do not have sufficient volume of export production to justify the expense of personal contact with the foreign buyers or to interest competent sales agencies.

One exporting manufactured products states:

The volume of business is so small that with the various companies acting independently instead of through an association, it is probable that no business would be obtained. Where competition is as keen as it is in our products, it is doubtful if foreign trade in these commodities could be carried on successfully except through an association.

The Small Producer.—Although the Export Trade Act was passed in war time it was not a simple war measure for its usefulness did not pass with the ending of the war. Rather, it becomes more and more important in peace time to the exporters of the nation who are engaged in a lively economic competition with the exporters of the other countries of the world. Cooperation among American small producers is especially advantageous. The great manufacturer of a specialty may proceed individually but the small producer needs to co-operate with others so that he may enjoy all the advantages of a powerful trust in the competition against the great combinations of foreign nations.[22]

America's Foreign Trade Position.—The past two decades, and especially the last ten years, have witnessed a great growth of interest in foreign trade in the United States. Americans have been entering seriously into foreign operations and have received aid from the Government by direct action in shipping, by permissive legislation in foreign banking expansion and export trade combination, and by excellent support through the reorganized Department of Commerce. At the end of the fiscal year, June 30, 1925, the United States had become the world's greatest exporting nation with Great Britain second and Germany and France ranking third and fourth. In total foreign trade the leading nations ranked as follows: United Kingdom, $10,736,238,000; United States, $8,688,788,000; Germany, $4,504,263,000; France, $4,233,938,000. The export trade of the United States, after adjustment was made to 1913 values, showed an increase of 31 per cent over the country's exports for the fiscal year ending June 30, 1913.

Having sketched the movement of American foreign trade since 1914, we may now examine the expansion of American foreign branch banks after that date.

---

[22] The trend toward combinations of exporters and combination of national interests in American foreign trade does not commend itself to many economists who see this tendency as a movement strongly tinged with neo-mercantilistic fallacies, advocating "unfair" methods in international competition, and leading to international distrust.

CHAPTER IX

THE EXPANSION OF AMERICAN FOREIGN
BRANCH BANKS SINCE 1914

The Extraordinary Expansion After 1914.—The countries of the world were dotted with the overseas branches of the great banks of foreign nations long before the first American banking institution established its first office abroad. But seldom, if ever, has there been such a striking growth of foreign branch bank organization as that which was experienced by American banking between the years 1914 and 1920. The first American foreign branch bank was established in 1887, but the movement toward foreign branch banking was very slow until after 1914. At the end of the year 1913 there were in existence only 6 foreign branches of American banking establishments doing a domestic business and 20 foreign offices of two American foreign banking corporations. By December 31, 1920 the foreign branches of American incorporated banking institutions had increased to 181,[1] not counting the 38 foreign branches of the American Express Company, Inc., which has since 1919 participated more and more in foreign banking operations. Of these 181 branches, 100 were the foreign offices of seven banks doing a regular banking business in the United States,[2] the other 81 belonging to five American foreign banking corporations.

---

[1] It would be difficult, and of doubtful value, to endeavor to fix any certain date as the day upon which the largest number of American branch banks were operating abroad. The great movement toward branch bank establishment culminated in 1920. From 1919 to 1920 American banks, especially the war-time foreign trade banks, were opening and closing branches on a great scale. The dates of authorization, actual opening and formal opening, and of formal closing and final closing differ appreciably, and so we find branches actually operating before the date of formal opening and others functioning for some time after formal announcement of withdrawal is given. The figure of approximately one hundred and eighty is believed to be substantially correct as indicating the top of the American foreign banking expansion. See p. 211.

[2] Twenty-nine of the 100 branches were the foreign offices of the National City Bank's subsidiary, the International Banking Corporation.

The war, of course, was the main factor in this notable expansion but the importance of the banking reforms of 1914 must not be overlooked. For if the World War provoked the expansion it is also true that the American banking reforms permitted it, granting our banking institutions full freedom to enter the foreign field without those legal restrictions to which they had previously been subject.

Later Withdrawals from Field.—When the period of abnormal trade occasioned by the war came to a close in 1920 and American foreign trade fell off nearly 50 per cent in value, it was evident that a large part of the American foreign branch banks called into existence by that trade would have to be withdrawn. From 1920 to 1925 there was a steady withdrawal of American banking institutions from the foreign field with the result that on June 30, 1926 the total number of American branch banks abroad, exclusive of 47 foreign branches of the American Express Company, Inc., was 107. All of these branch banks were owned by eight American banks doing a domestic business, 72 being direct branches, and 35 the branches of the subsidiary foreign banking corporations of two of the banks.[3] There were no longer any "independent" American foreign banking corporations in existence.

The expansion of American foreign branch banks will be treated in this chapter by first considering the expansion on the part of the American domestic banks and their subsidiaries, and then the expansion undertaken by the foreign banking corporations.

The Foreign Expansion of American Commercial Banks

The banking institutions commonly spoken of as American commercial banks are the national banks, the state banks, and

---

[3] The National City Bank of New York (France) S. A., the Paris subsidiary of the bank, is included here with the branches of subsidiary foreign banking corporations.

trust companies. Since 1887 when the Jarvis-Conklin Mortgage Trust Company established what appears to be the first
American foreign branch bank, eleven American institutions
doing a regular commercial banking business have established
or acquired foreign branches. These institutions will be considered in as far as possible in the chronological sequence of
the expansion movement.

The Equitable Trust Company of New York.—The Equitable Trust Company of New York [4] first opened its doors
for business on April 19, 1871 under the name of the Trader's
Deposit Company. Later the name of the company was
changed to the American Deposit and Loan Company, and
it was not until April 2, 1902 that the Equitable Trust Company of New York adopted its present designation, and extended its activities to include every banking and trust function
authorized by the laws of New York. On this date the capitalization of the bank was $1,000,000 as compared with an
authorized capital of $50,000 in 1871.

What is perhaps the oldest established foreign branch of
an American bank was opened as a one room office in London at 95 Gresham Street in 1887 by the Jarvis-Conklin Mortgage Trust Company. The parent concern closed its doors
during the panic of 1893 and was liquidated by the North
American Trust Company. The London office, however, was
continued, its activities increasing under the management of
the North American Trust Company. In 1905 the trust company changed its name to the Trust Company of America, and
when in 1912 the Equitable Trust Company of New York
purchased the Trust Company of America and its London
branch, attention was immediately focused on this branch.
A period of reconstruction and development set in, larger
space being taken at 3 King William Street. In this connec-

---

[4] Statement of condition on June 30, 1926: capital $30,000,000; surplus and un-
divided profits $21,468,392; deposits $408,479,024; total resources $512,705,332.

tion it is interesting to note that the original managers of the one room office of the Jarvis-Conklin Mortgage Trust Company remained in charge through each successive change of control and finally became the London managers of the branch under the Equitable Trust Company. This branch is the largest foreign office of the company, does a full commercial banking, investment and trust business, and now occupies an entire building at 10 Moorgate, London. A second London branch was opened in June, 1923 in the Bush House at Aldwych, the city's shopping and theatre center, as a convenience for American tourists.

THE PARIS BRANCH.—The Equitable Trust Company has two other foreign branches, one at Mexico City and one in Paris. The Paris office was the first foreign branch to be established by the company, being opened in May, 1910 in a building at the corner of the Rue de la Paix and the Avenue de l'Opera. Only three or four small rooms were occupied at first, the branch doing but little banking business and functioning mainly as an information bureau for clients of the bank visiting or living in Paris. At this time the office force consisted of a treasurer, a cashier, a stenographer, and a porter who served also as messenger boy. About three or four years later the office began to engage in general banking operations, specializing in deposits, investments, letters of credit, and French and foreign securities. During the year 1914 the office force was increased to 15 people.

When the World War came, the greater part of the employes of the branch was mobilized by the French Government, leaving only four persons to carry on the business. For several weeks the branch, like the other American institutions in Paris, was the scene of feverish activity, striving to meet the needs of Americans stranded in Paris who were trying to cash their letters of credit in order to settle their affairs and leave for the United States. The Equitable branch had taken precautions in time, as did the other American banks in

Europe, and did not take advantage of the moratorium, being able to meet the demands of all depositors and to cash all the various letters of credit presented.

During the years 1915 and 1916 the business of the branch grew and in order to take care of the French war loans and to undertake the reorganization of certain American securities the personnel was increased to 50. With the entry of the United States into the war, the branch became still more active, opening accounts for large numbers of the American Expeditionary Force and receiving very important accounts from the various army divisions and services, from the American Red Cross, the Y.M.C.A., and other American organizations in France. In 1918, the office force of the branch mounted to 200.

Since the end of the war the Paris branch has grown steadily in prestige and under able management is constantly expanding and increasing its facilities. Today with some 200 odd employes the branch is one of the important financial institutions of the French capital. Among the 47 banks in the Paris clearing house, the branch has ranked from twelfth to fourth in clearings since 1924.[5]

THE MEXICO CITY BRANCH.—For a number of years the Equitable Trust Company has been directly represented in Mexico. But it was not until January, 1921 that its office in Mexico City was converted into an institution established and formally registered under the laws of that country. The main functions of the Mexico City branch are to deal in foreign exchange and bullion, and to handle collections.

THE EQUITABLE EASTERN BANKING CORPORATION.—In December, 1920 the Equitable Trust Company created a subsidiary, the Equitable Eastern Banking Corporation, under the laws of the State of New York governing foreign banking corporations. The corporation which has a capitalization of $2,000,000 was formed for the purpose of taking over the

---

[5] The other American branch banks at Paris (Bankers Trust Company, Guaranty Trust Company, and National City Bank of New York) have also stood high, ranking usually in the highest third of the list.

company's Far Eastern business and opened its first foreign branch in Shanghai on January 2, 1921.[6] This branch was formerly a representative's office of the Equitable Trust Company. A second branch was established in Hongkong on January 2, 1925. The Equitable Eastern Banking Corporation is very ably managed and has pursued a sane and conservative policy since its foundation. In 1921, the first year of operation, it paid dividends at the rate of 6 per cent and since 1922 it has paid at the rate of 8 per cent per annum.[7] The corporation is one of the world's largest dealers in bullion.

GROWTH OF EQUITABLE TRUST COMPANY.—The Equitable Trust Company has experienced remarkable growth since its incorporation in 1902. At that time the officers and clerical force of the company numbered about 23, and the capital stock amounted to $1,000,000. In 1926 there were some 1,645 officers and employes in the New York offices alone, and the capital, surplus and undivided profits of the company had reached some $51,000,000. About fifteen years ago the company conducted a series of important mergers resulting in a notable growth. A late merger, and one of the most important, was completed on June 29, 1923 when the Importers and Traders National Bank became a part of the Equitable Trust Company organization. The company has not made a policy of retaining as branches the buildings of banks acquired, and has only three domestic branch banks. One of these is at 247 Broadway (the former Importers and Traders National Bank) and the others are located at 79 Madison Avenue and at Madison Avenue and Forty-fifth Street, New York City.

The Guaranty Trust Company of New York.—The Guaranty Trust Company of New York [8] was organized on April

---

[6] Some banks on the Pacific coast which were interested in operating with the Orient also participated in the creation of the corporation. Only one outside bank, the Citizens National Bank of Los Angeles, holds any stock in the Equitable Trust Company's subsidiary at present.

[7] Condition on August 31, 1926: capital $2,000,000; surplus $500,000; undivided profits $716,738; deposits $4,562,000; total resources $16,636,918.

[8] Condition on June 30, 1926: capital $25,000,000; surplus $20,000,000; undivided profits $3,250,452; deposits $519,987,524; total resources $644,502,758.

13, 1864, when the legislature of New York passed an act incorporating the New York Guaranty and Indemnity Company. In December, 1895 the supreme court in New York authorized this company to assume the name "Guaranty Trust Company of New York" on and after January 2, 1896. The object of the change in the name was to indicate, by the company's title, the exact nature of its business.

As a New York trust company, the institution had the right to establish foreign branches long before the state banking law was revised in 1914 permitting state banks as well as trust companies to install branches abroad. The company, however, established only one foreign branch before the entrance of the United States into the World War. This office was opened at 33 Lombard Street, London, on March 1, 1897. When it became evident that the United States would inevitably be drawn into the war, the company realized the imperative need for efficient banking connections between America and the Allied Nations in Europe to finance the export of war materials to the continent, to offer adequate banking facilities to American overseas forces, and to aid in future reconstruction. The company, therefore, opened an additional emergency office in London for the use of American troops, and sent a representative to France who opened an office at Paris in December, 1916. This office was formally opened as a branch on July 1, 1917. In 1919, three branches were established abroad: one in Liverpool, England; one in Brussels, Belgium; and one at Havre, France. In 1920 one branch was located in Pall Mall, London, and another at Constantinople. A third regular London branch was opened in Kingsway in 1921, and a branch at Antwerp, Belgium was installed on September 1, of that year. The Guaranty Trust Company established in all, nine regular foreign branches.

THE PARIS BRANCH.—The most important foreign branch of the Guaranty Trust Company of New York is the Lombard Street office in London. The Paris office also does a large volume of business and serves a particularly important group of Americans living or traveling abroad. This office was opened on December 5, 1916 at 4 Rue Edouard–VII in an apartment on the third floor with a force consisting of a representative of the company and three clerks. Its first great French industrial loan was negotiated in America from these quarters. On July 1, 1917 the branch was officially opened in its present location at 1 & 3 Rue des Italiens with a force of 34 employes who worked under difficult conditions, the building not being completely finished until the spring of 1918. An important part of the business of the branch at the beginning was the opening of accounts for American officers and men in France, and a special sub-branch of the Paris office was opened at Tours in June, 1918 for this purpose. The Paris branch of the Guaranty Trust Company adopted a vigorous policy from the very beginning and had a rapid and successful growth. On June 1, 1925 its force numbered 265 making the branch, from the point of view of personnel, the largest of the company's foreign offices.

DOMESTIC BRANCHES.—The Guaranty Trust Company has two domestic branch offices. The Fifth Avenue office, now at the corner of 44th Street, was opened following the merger with the Fifth Avenue Trust Company in January, 1910.[9] The other, at Madison Avenue and 60th Street, New York City, was installed on January 2, 1918. The company has no foreign representatives. Eight of the nine regular foreign branches which have been established by the Guaranty Trust Company of New York are still functioning, and are firmly seated in their respective markets. The special agencies opened in London and at Tours for the convenience of American troops were discontinued after the armistice, and the Constantinople branch was closed in 1922. The company has made the greatest foreign expansion of any American trust company.

---

[9] The Guaranty Trust Company absorbed the Fifth Avenue Trust Company and the Morton Trust Company in 1910, and the Standard Trust Company in 1912.

The Farmers' Loan and Trust Company.—The Farmers' Loan and Trust Company,[10] New York City, is one of the oldest banking institutions in the United States. It was organized under the laws of the State of New York in 1822, and was one of the first American banks to establish foreign branches. The company opened two branches in 1906, one in London and one at Paris. These two European branches were of great service to the United States during the World War.

THE LONDON BRANCH.—The London branch remained open during the moratorium which was taken advantage of by the banks in that center, and was able to take care of its own customers as well as all Americans who applied with proper credentials. After about six weeks most of the Americans in England had been enabled to get home. Then the branch started in earnest upon its war work. It was appointed by the British Government as trustee in connection with its first secured loan of $250,000,000 in the United States. The branch was then named by the United States Government as bankers in London of the United States Navy. This became the most important war work of the office since the principal disbursements of the United States Navy in European waters during the war went through the branch. Credits were opened at various points on the continent on behalf of the United States Navy officials, and naval officers and men were enabled to remit funds to their homes in America. For a long period during the war the branch also had the London banking accounts of the United States War Trade Board and the United States Food Administration until the closing of the London offices of these organizations.

THE PARIS BRANCH.—The Paris branch, being so close to the war zone, was especially helpful to American citizens and organizations in France. It remained open during the moratorium declared in Paris, as did the other American banks in

---

[10] Condition on June 30, 1926: capital $10,000,000; surplus and undivided profits $19,493,103; deposits $143,408,541; total resources $182,005,416.

that center, and the numerous Americans seeking funds were taken care of so that by the end of August most American citizens were safely out of the country and homeward bound. The staff of the branch had been cut to two employes by the French mobilization: a bookkeeper and a woman stenographer, but it carried on during the strenuous period when Paris was filled with Americans trying to cash letters of credit or to secure money in some way for passage home. The branch had placed itself in a strong position before the moratorium was established on August 2, 1914. During the latter part of July as the war approached there were runs on all the banks in France and transfers no longer being possible through the ordinary exchange channels, the cashier of the branch went to the St. Lazare railroad station every morning with a porter to get a case containing bags of a thousand sovereigns each sent over by the London branch. In this way an emergency fund was built up to serve American travelers.

EXPANSION OF SUB-AGENCIES IN FRANCE.—During 1915 and 1916 there was a great development of the business of the Paris branch. It played an important part in financial operations connected with American exports to France, in the French war loans, and as banker for the ambulance, relief and flying organizations of the United States. At the beginning of 1917, the office force had increased to 75 people, and the deposits had mounted to 30,000,000 francs (about $6,000,000). The branch then prepared to open sub-branches at the ports where American forces would land and at their training camps. These sub-agencies were located at St. Nazaire (July 23, 1917), Bordeaux (August 16, 1917), and Neufchâteau (September 20, 1917). The offices extended banking facilities to American officers and men, exchanging money, encouraging saving, and transferring funds back home. The branch at Paris made many thousands of cable and mail transfers to the United States during the first year of the American Expeditionary Force in France, and carried a great list of company

funds, hospital funds, and accounts with paymasters and secre-
taries of all the relief organizations.

In 1918 the Bordeaux agency had deposits of 10,000,000
francs and the office force of the Paris branch had increased to
200. The Paris office was appointed one of the special agencies
in Paris for the convenience of United States Army paymasters, and its business from army organizations and men
grew steadily. Arrangements were made with one of the
great French banks, the Société Générale, to open accounts at
the bank's local branch in all towns where large numbers of
American troops were stationed, and in this way the Farmers'
Loan and Trust Company extended its service to every place
where it was needed.

THE PRESENT ORGANIZATION.—As the American troops
withdrew from France after the armistice and the various
American organizations left, the sub-agencies were closed, the
Neufchâteau and St. Nazaire agencies in March and April,
1919 and the Bordeaux office in December, 1919. Two years
later, on December 31, 1921 the Farmers' Loan and Trust
Company liquidated its Paris branch, the office being taken
over by the National City Bank of New York which still maintains it at 41 Boulevard Hausmann. Since this time the company has maintained a representative's office in the Banque
de Paris et des Pays-Bas at Paris. The London branch of the
Farmers' Loan and Trust Company has never endeavored to
compete with the large English banking interests, and while
its volume of business has been gradual in its growth, it has
been satisfactory. The company has two domestic branches at
475 Fifth Avenue and 901 Madison Avenue in New York City,
and an office on board the S. S. *Leviathan*.

The Empire Trust Company.—The Empire Trust Company,[11] New York City, was organized under the laws of the

---

[11] Condition on June 30, 1926: capital $4,000,000; surplus and undivided profits
$4,001,207; deposits $82,360,735; total resources $90,841,702.

State of New York in 1902 and has had a very rapid growth during the past decade. The bank has established only one foreign branch. This is the London office which was originally opened at 9 New Broad Street in June, 1913. One year later it was removed to 41 Threadneedle Street where it remained until November 24, 1924 upon which date it was transferred to 28 Charles Street, its present location. The company has two domestic branches in New York City. The Fifth Avenue branch was established in 1906 at 487 Fifth Avenue, and in February, 1913 was removed to the Empire Trust Company building at 580 Fifth Avenue. The Hudson branch at 1411 Broadway was formerly the main office of the Hudson Trust Company and became a branch of the Empire Trust Company upon its absorption of the former company in June, 1924.

The National City Bank of New York.—The only American bank having a world system of foreign branches is the National City Bank of New York, "the greatest bank in the Western Hemisphere." This institution which was established in 1812 is one of the oldest American banks, and it is the most important commercial bank in the United States.[12]

The National City Bank of New York may be said to be the descendant of the First Bank of the United States. The First Bank, in which the United States Government owned one-fifth of the capital stock, operated from 1791 to 1811 when its charter expired. Congress refused to recharter the bank and a group of prominent citizens organized the City Bank of New York to fill the gap left by the loss of the first Bank of the United States. The directors arranged for the exchange of shares of the First Bank stock for shares of City Bank stock and this was so well accepted that a majority of the stock was subscribed for. Thus it may be said that in this

---

[12] Condition on June 30, 1926: capital $50,000,000; surplus $50,000,000; undivided profits $13,133,488; deposits $963,554,075; total resources $1,281,494,453.

way the National City Bank of New York is the direct off-spring of the First Bank of the United States. The City Bank of New York became the National City Bank of New York upon entrance to the National banking system created in 1864 by the National-Bank Act. Being a national bank, it was prohibited from establishing foreign branches until 1914, but after the passage of the Federal Reserve Act authorizing national banks to install branches in foreign countries, it immediately proceeded to the establishment of a net of offices in certain foreign markets.

BANK'S FOREIGN EXPANSION.—The first foreign branch of the National City Bank was opened at Buenos Aires, Argentina on November 10, 1914. In 1915 five more branches were installed. Three of these were in Brazil at Rio de Janeiro, Santos, and Sao Paulo; the others were at Montevideo, Uruguay, and Havana, Cuba. In this same year the bank made the most important step in the early development of its system of foreign branches when it acquired the International Banking Corporation with a head office at 60 Wall Street, New York and branches in London and San Francisco and in nearly all the important ports of the Orient.

Four branches were opened in 1916: Santiago, Cuba; Bahia, Brazil; Valparaiso, Chile; and Genoa, Italy. In 1917 branches were established at Petrograd and Moscow in Russia and at Caracas, Venezuela. Only two branches were opened in 1918, one at San Juan, Porto Rico and one at Santiago, Chile, but in 1919, which was the year of the bank's greatest foreign expansion, thirty-three foreign branches were established. This was the first year of the post-war boom which was to end in the world crisis of 1920. Twenty-two branches were installed in Cuba: Cienfuegos, Matanzas, Sagua la Grande, Cárdenas, Camagüey, Guantánamo, Manzanillo, Cuatro Caminos (Havana), Caibarién, Galiano (Havana), Artemisa, Santa Clara, Unión de Reyes, Pinar del Rio, Ciego de Ávila, Remedios, Yagüajay, Bayamo, Cruces, Colón, Sancti Spiritus, and Placetas del Norte. Two were located in Brazil, at Pernambuco and Porto Alegre; two in Argentina, at Rosario and Once (Buenos Aires), and one each at Port of Spain, Trinidad; Maracaibo, Venezuela; Barcelona, Spain; Calle Rondeau, Uruguay; Medellín, Colombia; Brussels, Belgium; and Vladivostok, Russia.

WITHDRAWALS BEGIN.—Eleven more branches were opened in 1920. Two of these were in Colombia, at Barranquilla and Bogotá; two in London; and the others were located at Antwerp, Belgium; Cape Town, South Africa; Ponce, Porto Rico; Ciudad Bolivar, Venezuela; Nuevitas, Cuba; Lima, Peru; and Madrid, Spain. During 1920 two branches were closed. These were at Maracaibo and Ciudad Bolivar in Venezuela. The Madrid and Barcelona branches were transferred to the International Banking Corporation at the end of the year. In 1921 no new branches were established but five were withdrawn: Bahia, Brazil; Once, Argentina; Port of Spain, Trinidad; Porto Alegre, Brazil; and Cape Town, South Africa. In 1922 the Paris branch of the Farmers' Loan and Trust Company was acquired, and five foreign offices were closed: Unión de Reyes and Cruces in Cuba and Medellín, Barranquilla and Bogotá in Colombia. Two branches were installed in Cuba at Florida and La Lonja (Havana) in 1923, and four offices located at Artemisa, Colón and Placetas del Norte in Cuba and at Ponce, Porto Rico were closed. In 1924 the branch at Calle Rondeau, Uruguay was closed and since that year no foreign branches have been withdrawn by the National City Bank.

The bank's statement for December 31, 1924 declared that, "The foreign branches have everywhere been profitable during the year, the net earnings from this source being nearly 80 per cent in excess of those of the year 1923." In Cuba, where the business of the branches had been very satisfactory and had indicated substantial progress, eight fine bank buildings were acquired and a new bank building was completed in Havana to provide for the increasing business in 1924.

THE BANK OF HAITI.—In 1925 the bank established three new branches: one at Milan, Italy, and two at Moron and Vertientes in Cuba, and took over seven of the eight branches in Santo Domingo of its subsidiary, the International Banking Corporation, making them its own direct branches.[13]   In this year the bank also acquired control of the entire capital stock of the Banque Nationale de la République d'Haiti whose profitable operations had been under the guidance of the bank for several years.   The Banque de la République d'Haiti opened for business on September 15, 1922 and now has ten branches in the principal ports of the island.   Under its contract of concession it is the government bank of issue and as the fiscal agent of the Haitian Government it receives and pays out all funds of the government.   The entire capital stock, outside of qualifying director's shares, is owned by the Bank of Haiti, Inc., whose capital stock in turn is owned by the National City Bank of New York.[14]

The report of the National City Bank for 1925 stated:

The extension of our business abroad, especially with respect to our foreign branches, has continued during the year, and this section of our business has returned profits exceeding those of the previous year by nearly twenty per cent.   The contacts made through institutional activity in foreign fields, and the knowledge of foreign markets thus gained, have proved of unquestioned value to American manufacturers and merchants seeking foreign markets, and to American travelers who have used our letters of credit and travelers' checks in greater volume than ever before, and they have made it possible for us to be of increasing assistance everywhere in the transaction of international trade and commerce.

DEVELOPMENT OF THE BANK'S FOREIGN BRANCH POLICY. —Early in 1926 the National City Bank took over from the International Banking Corporation the subsidiary's two

---

[13] One of the corporation's branches, at Sanchez, was closed in 1925.

[14] Condition of the Banque Nationale de la République d'Haiti of Port-au-Prince, Haiti, on December 31, 1925: capital authorized $2,000,000; capital paid in $1,600,000; surplus $150,000; undivided profits 19,894; circulation $3,357,194; deposits $6,730,277; total assets $12,546,233.

branches in the Republic of Panama, one in the city of Panama established in 1904, and one at Colon established in 1906. These branches were the only ones the corporation had left in the Western Hemisphere after the transfer of its Santo Domingo branches to the bank. The development of the policy —more efficient administration through *direct* branches—continues. In 1927, the bank will take over the 17 branches in the Orient of the corporation, leaving the latter only 5 foreign branches: London, Barcelona, Madrid, Manila and Cebu.

Of the total of sixty-four branches established by the National City Bank, seventeen were closed; two were transferred to the bank's subsidiary; and three are inactive.[15] Nine branches were taken over from the bank's subsidiary, the International Banking Corporation and one (the Paris branch, later changed into a subsidiary) was acquired from the Farmers' Loan and Trust Company. Thus in 1926 the National City Bank's foreign organization was represented by: (a) Fifty-one direct branches located as follows: Argentina, two; Belgium, two; Brazil, four; Chile, two; Cuba, twenty-four; England, two; Italy, two; Panama, two; Peru, one; Porto Rico, one; Santo Domingo, seven; Uruguay, one; Venezuela, one; (b) one domestic subsidiary, the International Banking Corporation, with twenty-two branches established as follows: China, eight; England, one; India, three; Japan, four; Java, one; Philippine Islands, two; Spain, two; Straits Settlements, one; (c) two foreign subsidiary banks, the National City Bank of New York (France) S.A., and the Banque Nationale de la République d'Haiti with ten branches in Haiti.

DOMESTIC BRANCHES.—Having thoroughly established its foreign organization, the National City Bank is active in the extension of its business in the metropolitan area of New York now made possible through the sanction by the government of the establishment of domestic branch offices by national banks. In 1925 it had seven branches in New York City, and in March

---

[15] The three Russian branches of the bank.

1926 it purchased the Peoples Trust Company of Brooklyn thus acquiring eleven more branches in Greater New York.[16]

At this point, the foreign expansion of the National City Bank having been considered at some length, the growth of the International Banking Corporation may be studied. The corporation is taken up here rather than in the section upon foreign banking corporations because since 1915 it has not been an independent enterprise but a subsidiary owned by the National City Bank of New York.

The International Banking Corporation.—The International Banking Corporation,[17] New York City, was the first American banking institution to establish a system of foreign branches. It began its operations in 1902 under a charter of very broad scope granted by the State of Connecticut in 1901. The corporation was organized principally in consequence of the conquest of the Philippines on the theory that the possession of the islands would open the way to a large American participation in the China trade and in the railway development of that country. Soon it became apparent that the trade of China was so linked up with that of other Eastern countries that branches in Japan, Straits Settlements, and India were a practical necessity, and such branches were opened as rapidly as a skilled staff, largely recruited from British colonial banks, could be secured. Subsequently branches were installed in the Isthmus of Panama as an aid to the United States Government in connection with the construction of the Panama Canal, and in Santo Domingo.

Pre-War Expansion.—By 1914, the International Banking Corporation had opened seventeen branches in foreign countries. These branches were located as follows: five in

---

[16] The Peoples Trust Company, founded in 1889, was one of the oldest and largest banking institutions in Brooklyn. On January 15, 1926 it reported its condition as follows; capital $2,000,000; surplus and undivided profits $5,135,748; deposits $67,860,584; total assets $76,047,628.

[17] Condition on June 30, 1926; capital $5,000,000; surplus $5,000,000; undivided profits $4,504,146; deposits $79,724, 717; total resources $124,967,285.

China: Shanghai 1902, Hongkong 1903, Canton 1904, Hankow 1909, and Peking 1909; one in England at London in 1902; two in India: Bombay 1903, and Calcutta 1904; two in Japan: Yokohama 1902, and Kobe 1904; two in the Philippines: Manila 1902, and Cebu 1905; two in Panama: Panama City 1904, and Colon 1906; two in the Straits Settlements: Singapore 1902, and Penang 1904; one in Mexico City in 1903. Two of these foreign branches were closed: the Mexico City agency in 1914, and the Penang office in 1908. Thus before the great American war trade began the International Banking Corporation possessed fifteen branches in foreign countries.[18]

WAR AND POST-WAR EXPANSION.—Between 1914 and 1926 the corporation established nineteen branches, acquired two from the National City Bank, and transferred nine to the bank. In 1916, two branches were installed, one at Tientsin, China, and one at Medellín, Colombia. Four branches were opened in 1917, all being located in Santo Domingo at Puerta Plata, San Pedro de Macoris, Santiago de los Caballeros and Santo Domingo City. In 1918 two new branches were established, both in Java, at Batavia and Sourabaya. 1919 was the year of greatest expansion when five branches were opened. Two of these were in China at Harbin and Tsingtao, one in Santo Domingo at Sanchez, one in France at Lyon, and one in India at Rangoon. In 1920 two more branches were established in Santo Domingo at Barahona and San Francisco de Macoris. The Madrid and Barcelona branches of the National City Bank were acquired on January 1, 1921 and a branch was installed at La Vega in Santo Domingo during the year. This was the eighth office to be opened in the Dominican Republic by the International Banking Corporation. The corporation established these branches at the instance of the United States Government and entered into a contract whereby it became the

---

[18] The corporation has also established branches in the United States, one at San Francisco in 1902 and one at Washington, D. C., in 1903. The latter branch was closed in 1912.

fiscal agent of the Dominican Government. In 1923, the corporation established two branches, one at Dairen in China and one at Tokyo, Japan, and in 1925 another branch was opened in Japan at Osaka, an important manufacturing center of that country. In 1925, as previously noted, the corporation transferred seven of its Dominican branches to the National City Bank, closing the remaining one at Sanchez, and in 1926 it transferred its two Panama branches to the bank.

Five branches were closed between 1914 and 1926: Medellín, Colombia in 1919; Tsingtao, China in 1921; Lyon, France in 1923; Sourabaya, Java in 1924; and Sanchez, Santo Domingo in 1925. The International Banking Corporation, since its organization in 1901, has established in all thirty-six foreign branches and acquired two. Of this total of thirty-eight branches only seven have been closed, and nine were taken over by the National City Bank. In 1926 the International Banking Corporation had a staff of employes numbering over 1,400 and possessed twenty-two branch banks in eight foreign countries.

The Commercial National Bank.—The Commercial National Bank was chartered April 19, 1904 and is one of the well-known banking establishments of Washington, D. C. After the organization of the Federal Reserve System the Commercial National Bank made preparations for foreign expansion and applied to the Federal Reserve Board on January 8, 1915 for permission to locate offices in Panama at Panama City and Cristóbal. The possibility of securing some government business was very probably a consideration underlying this policy. The bank opened both branches in 1915 but sold them in April, 1918 to the American Foreign Banking Corporation. The capital, surplus and undivided profits of the Commercial National Bank amount to a little less than one and one half million dollars making it the smallest American bank that has established foreign branches.

The First National Bank of Boston.—The direct ancestor of the First National Bank of Boston [19] was the famous Massachusetts Bank which was founded February 7, 1784. The First National Bank of Boston received its charter under the national banking laws in 1864, and was financing a large amount of trade with South America before the war, but being a national bank it was prohibited from establishing any foreign branches.

The volume of trade between certain South American ports and New England naturally led the bank to desire to install branches in those ports. For example, Buenos Aires was sending to Boston great quantities of wool, hides and skins, quebracho, linseed, and the like, while Boston firms were selling finished products such as shoes, textiles, and machinery to Argentine merchants. Cuba was also a great market for New England manufactures, in fact it has been the best in recent years, exporting in return sugar, tobacco, and fruits in great quantities. Without branches in these countries the First National Bank of Boston was getting only a part of the profitable banking business arising from their trade with New England. When the Federal Reserve Act was passed the bank studied the situation carefully and decided to enter the Argentine and Cuban markets.

TWO FOREIGN BRANCHES.—The first foreign branch of the bank was established in Buenos Aires at Bartomlomé Mitre 501 on July 14, 1917. The business of the branch grew rapidly from the very first and in 1924 it was transferred to new quarters at Florida 99. This is the finest bank and office building in all South America and was built by the First National Bank of Boston as an example of the best modern Spanish architecture. The second foreign branch of the bank was opened in August, 1923 in the Pedro Gomez Mena building in Havana, Cuba. This branch, like the first, has been operating successfully since

---

[19] Condition on June 30, 1926: capital $20,000,000; surplus and undivided profits $24,120,935; deposits $305,349,079; total resources $397,844,826.

its establishment. Mr. Wing, president of the bank, returning from a trip to the foreign branches in 1925 was impressed with the "solidity and the potentialities of the expansion the First National Bank of Boston has made in the Argentine and Cuba." The deposit account in both countries was close to $50,000,000, of which between $40,000,000 and $42,000,000 were in Buenos Aires. "Despite the deflationary losses of 1920–1921 the First National has managed to make better than an average business return upon its investment in foreign banking." [20]

DOMESTIC BRANCHES.—In addition to the two foreign branches, the bank has an European representative's office, opened in September, 1922, at Gresham House, 24 Old Broad Street, London, and a total of seven branches and four sub-offices in Boston. An important part of the growth of the bank has been due to mergers with other banks. On June 27, 1903 the bank and the Massachusetts National Bank (formerly the Massachusetts Bank) were merged. May 1, 1904 marked the merger with the National Bank of Redemption which had previously absorbed the Everett, Blackstone, and Shoe & Leather National banks. On July 17, 1923 the bank absorbed the International Trust Company which had grown through the absorption of the Lincoln Trust, Old South Trust, Dorchester Trust, Hyde Park Trust, and Market Trust Companies. Of the eight bank buildings acquired by the First National Bank of Boston through merging, one was closed, the head office of the International Trust Company, and the other seven retained as branches. After 1923 the bank opened four additional offices.

The Bankers Trust Company.—The Bankers Trust Company, New York City, is one of the youngest and yet one of the great American banks. Incorporated under the laws of the State of New York on March 30, 1903, it has had a remark-

---

[20] *Wall Street Journal*, December 23, 1925

able growth to a place of considerable power.[21] The Bankers
Trust Company was conceived by Henry Pomeroy Davison and
the members of its first board of directors were all bankers,
either officers of important banks or members of banking firms
in New York or elsewhere. To the new company they directed
trust business which at that time national banks were not allowed to handle. A substantial part of the company's growth
was due to the successive mergers with the Mercantile Trust
Company in 1911, the Manhattan Trust Company in 1912, and
the Astor Trust Company in 1917. Its business was almost
strictly confined to the operations of a trust company until its
entrance into the Federal Reserve System on October 19, 1917.

BRANCHES AT PARIS AND LONDON.—The bank has two
branches abroad, one at 3 and 5 Place Vendôme, Paris, opened
in June, 1920, and one at 26 Old Broad Street, London, established in September, 1924. The object of the company in
establishing branches in these cities was "to meet the requirements of business houses engaged in international trade; to
serve effectively the interests of correspondent banks, and to
provide adequate banking facilities for individuals resident or
traveling in Europe." The Bankers Trust Company, like other
great New York banks, has a great list of correspondents in
the United States, and it was convinced that its service to its
correspondents could be made most effective only by establishing branches in the leading European centers.

DOMESTIC BRANCHES.—In addition to its foreign branches,
the Bankers Trust Company has two branches in New York
City, one at Fifth Avenue and 42nd Street and the other at
Madison Avenue and 57th Street. The company's offices, both
domestic and foreign, are "complete, self-contained banking
units," and "are never spoken of or considered as branches."
Actually, however, they are no more nor less than direct
branches of the parent bank at 16 Wall Street.

---

[21] The first statement for June 30, 1903 showed: capital $1,000,000; surplus
$500,000; undivided profits $2,851; deposits $5,748,174; total resources $7,258,526. The
statement for June 30, 1926 showed: capital $20,000,000; surplus $20,000,000; undivided profits $13,043,867; deposits $426,246,963; total resources $545,749,317.

The Chase National Bank of New York.—The Chase National Bank of the City of New York,[22] is one of the newcomers into the field of foreign branch banking. The bank was established in 1877 and "named for the father of all national banks, Salmon P. Chase." Prior to 1914 it was unable to establish branches abroad due to the prohibition against branch banking by national banks, but even after the passage of the Federal Reserve Act it established no foreign offices although it was the second largest national bank in the United States. However, in 1917, the bank took part with a number of other American banks in the organization of the American Foreign Banking Corporation. This corporation established a number of foreign branches (page 156) but closed all but three: Havana, Cuba; Panama City, Panama; and Cristobal, Panama, when it was taken over by the Chase National Bank on January 12, 1925. These branches are now being maintained by the bank. At the time of purchase the deposits of the three branches amounted to $9,479,000, on June 30, 1925 they totaled $10,743,000, and have continued to show substantial increase.

On April 12, 1926 the Chase National Bank absorbed the Mechanics and Metals National Bank, New York, thereby increasing its capital from $20,000,000 to $40,000,000 and its total assets from $638,050,230 to $918,915,628, and acquiring thirteen more domestic branches in addition to the seven it possessed.[23] The merger maintained the Chase National Bank's position as a close rival of the National City Bank of New York, the largest commercial banking institution in the United States.

---

[22] Condition on June 30, 1926: capital $40,000,000; surplus $25,000,000; undivided profits $11,764,122; deposits $813,425,869; total resources $931,650,714.

[23] The Mechanics and Metals National Bank was established in 1810. It began as the first laborers' bank in the United States, its original directorate being chosen chiefly from members of the central society of mechanics and tradesmen. Before its absorption by the Chase National Bank it presented the following condition: capital $10,000,000; surplus and undivided profits $16,134,300; deposits $332,507,370; total assets $308,761,214. The 13 domestic branches acquired from the Mechanics and Metals National Bank are being maintained by the Chase National Bank.

The Foreign Expansion of American Foreign Banking Corporations

Foreign Trade Banks.—The foreign expansion of the International Banking Corporation, established long before the World War, and of the Equitable Eastern Banking Corporation, established after the close of the post-war boom, has been notably successful. These corporations have been treated in considering the foreign expansion of the banks of which they are subsidiaries, the National City Bank and the Equitable Trust Company respectively. There have been six other American foreign banking corporations which were not subsidiaries of any one American bank, but were enterprises formed by a large number of American interests. These corporations, with one exception, were established as a result of the war. They were unfortunate and have all passed out of existence. Before closing this section, the American Express Company Inc., which has engaged to a great extent in foreign banking operations since its creation in 1919, will be mentioned.

The Continental Banking and Trust Company of Panama.—The Continental Banking and Trust Company of Panama was incorporated May 29, 1913 under the laws of the State of West Virginia governing non-resident domestic corporations. The corporation represented West Virginia capitalists and was capitalized at $100,000 at the outset. On September 23, 1913 the capitalization was raised to $1,000,000. Foreign branches were established in Panama at David, Bocas del Toro, and Chorillo, and in Colombia at Santa Marta. The corporation functioned for several years and then entered into voluntary liquidation being dissolved by decree of the court of July 11, 1922.

The Mercantile Bank of the Americas.—The Mercantile Bank of the Americas was organized on August 10, 1915 under the laws of the State of Connecticut with an authorized capital of $25,000,000 by Brown Brothers and Company, J. and W. Seligman and Company, and a number of other American interests. It established direct branches in Europe at Paris, Barcelona, Madrid, and Hamburg, but its foreign expansion was principally made through its creation of affiliated corporations under the laws of Connecticut. These corporations were organized for banking in particular Latin American countries upon the theory that since the countries differ with regard to banking laws, currency, and customs, a separate corporation should be formed to operate within each country. In each case the corporation was under joint American and local management but the Mercantile Bank of the Americas held all or at least 51 per cent of the stock. The corporations could hardly be called subsidiaries for, although in some cases the Mercantile Bank of the Americas owned 100 per cent of the stock, the management was divided. They are usually referred to as affiliates, and will be so named here, but it must be understood that they were the commandite form of affiliate, the Mercantile Bank of the Americas controlling in every case the stock of the corporations.

The American Mercantile Bank of Peru was the first of the affiliated corporations to be organized and was incorporated May 29, 1916 with an authorized capital of $5,000,000. It established offices in Peru at Lima, Arequipa, Chiclayo, Callao, Piura, and Trujillo. The American Mercantile Bank of Caracas, founded October 3, 1917 with an authorized capital of $2,000,000, installed offices in Venezuela at Caracas, La Guayra, Maracaibo, Puerto Cabello, and Valencia. The American Mercantile Bank of Colombia, established January 19, 1918 with an authorized capital of $2,000,000, located offices in Colombia at Bogotá, Barranquilla, Cartagena, Medellín, Cali, Girardot, Manizales, Honda, Armenia, Bucaramanga, and Cúcuta. The American Mercantile Bank of Brazil established offices at Para and Pernambuco, and the American Mercantile

Bank of Cuba located offices at Havana and Ciego de Ávilla. The Banco Mercantil de Costa Rica with one office in San José became an affiliate of the Mercantile Bank of the Americas in 1917. Later the National Bank of Nicaragua with offices at Managua, Bluefields, León, and Granada, and the Banco Atlántida (Honduras) with offices at La Ceiba, Tegucigalpa, San Pedro Sula, Puerto Cortez, Tela, and Amapala also became affiliated with the Mercantile Bank of the Americas.

The Mercantile Bank of the Americas had one domestic branch at New Orleans, and was owner of the Mercantile Overseas Corporation which had one branch in Ecuador, one in Venezuela, and two in Colombia, and representatives in Europe. In all, the bank possessed forty-one foreign banking offices through its affiliates and four direct foreign branches.

This note on the activities of the Mercantile Bank of the Americas indicates the extensive nature of the bank's expansion. The marked decline in the prices of coffee, sugar, cocoa and other South American products after the crisis of 1920 made it impossible for the bank's customers to meet their obligations, and as a result of its losses the bank closed its European branches and disposed of the stock of its affiliated institutions at the end of 1921. In 1922, the bank was reorganized as the Bank of Central and South America.[24]

The American Foreign Banking Corporation.—The American Foreign Banking Corporation was incorporated in June, 1917 under New York State laws and stock was subscribed for by some thirty-four banking institutions throughout the country and by one Canadian institution. The Corporation established seventeen foreign branches and acquired two others making its greatest expansion between January, 1919 and the end of 1920. Seven branches were located in Santo Domingo at La Vega, Puerto Plata, Sanchez, San Francisco de Marcoris, Santiago de los Caballeros, San Pedro

---

[24] See page 158.

de Macoris, and Santo Domingo City. The remaining twelve branches were at Brussels, Belgium; Buenos Aires, Argentina; Cali, Colombia; Cristóbal and Panama City, Panama;[25] Harbin, China; Havana, Cuba; Manila, Philippine Islands; Port-au-Prince, Haiti; Rio de Janeiro, Brazil; San Pedro Sula, Republic of Honduras; and Mexico City, Mexico.

The American Foreign Banking Corporation disposed of all its foreign branches except those at Havana, Panama City, Cristóbal, and Mexico City during 1922. The Mexico City branch was closed soon after, and the three remaining offices were acquired on January 12, 1925 by the Chase National Bank of New York which had participated in the organization of the Corporation.[26]

The Asia Banking Corporation.—The Asia Banking Corporation was organized under the laws of New York State on August 9, 1918 with a capital stock of $2,000,000 by the Guaranty Trust Company, New York City, and later stock was sold to the Bankers' Trust Company of New York, the Continental and Commercial Bank of Chicago, the Guardian Savings and Trust Company of Cleveland and other American interests. The corporation opened in all eleven foreign branches and one domestic branch office. Six foreign branches were authorized by the banking department of New York State in 1918: Vladivostok, Russia and Harbin, Shanghai, Hankow, Tientsin and Peking in China. The first two branches were not opened. In 1919 four branches were installed, one at Manila, Philippine Islands and three in China at Changsha, Hongkong and Canton. A domestic office was opened in 1920 at San Francisco and a foreign branch installed at Singapore, Straits Settlements. In 1921 a branch at Corregidor, Philippine Islands was authorized but not opened. A branch was located at Yokohama, Japan in 1922, and in

[25] The Cristobal and Panama City branches were acquired from the Commercial National Bank of Washington, D. C., in 1918.

[26] See page 153.

1923 the corporation's last foreign branch was established at Kyo-miachi (Kobe), Japan to take the place of the Yokohama office which was withdrawn.

The Asia Banking Corporation went into voluntary liquidation in the year 1924, selling the major part of its assets to the International Banking Corporation although not legally merged with that institution.[27]

The Park-Union Foreign Banking Corporation.—The Park-Union Foreign Banking Corporation was created in 1919 under New York laws by the National Park Bank of New York and the Union Bank of Canada for the purpose of financing trade between the United States and Canada and the Far East. The corporation established branches at Yokohama, Shanghai, Tokio, and Paris in 1919. Domestic branches were opened at San Francisco and Seattle. The corporation did not have much success, entering as it did into the foreign field just before the world crisis of 1920. In 1922 the corporation went into voluntary liquidation,[28] at the office of the Asia Banking Corporation.

The Bank of Central and South America.—The Bank of Central and South America was incorporated under the laws of the State of Connecticut on August 4, 1922 with an authorized capital of $5,000,000. J. P. Morgan and Company, the Guaranty Trust Company, Brown Brothers and Company, J. and W. Seligman and Company, the Corn Exchange Bank, the Mechanics and Metals National Bank, W. R. Grace and Company, and other interests were represented in this foreign banking corporation. It was the Mercantile Bank of the Americas reconstituted to operate on a more modest scale,

---

[27] Certified order of the court filed with the banking department of New York, April 30, 1924. The International Banking Corporation liquidated the business of the Asia Banking Corporation for the account of the stockholders of the latter.

[28] Certified copy of order of the court filed with the banking department of New York, November 21, 1922.

more than half the foreign offices of the latter bank having been withdrawn. Its foreign organization in 1922 consisted of one branch at Hamburg, Germany and twenty-two foreign offices owned through the following banks taken over from the Mercantile Bank of the Americas:

American Mercantile Bank of Caracas (100 per cent stock owned) with offices at Caracas, La Guayra, Maracaibo, and Valencia in Venezuela.

American Mercantile Bank of Peru (99.9 per cent stock owned) with offices at Lima, Arequipa, Callao, Chiclayo, Piura, and Trujillo.

American Mercantile Bank of Colombia (100 per cent stock owned) with offices at Medellín, Barranquilla, Bogotá, Cali, Cartagena, Girardot, and Manizales.

National Bank of Nicaragua (51 per cent stock owned —49 per cent by Government of Nicaragua) with offices in Managua, Bluefields, León and Granada.

Banco Mercantil de Costa Rica (82.26 per cent stock owned—remainder by local people) with one office at San José.

Liquidation and Sale of Branches to Royal Bank of Canada.—The Bank of Central and South America operated a little over two years when it was decided to liquidate, and the corporation was sold to the Royal Bank of Canada on February 3, 1925. With the purchase of the Bank of Central and South America, the Royal Bank of Canada acquired the branches of the organizations in Colombia, Venezuela, Costa Rica, and Peru with the exception of the Callao and Arequipa branches of the Mercantile Bank of Peru which had been closed. Sixteen banking establishments in all were thus taken over to be converted into branches of the Royal Bank of Canada. The remainder of the assets of the Mercantile Bank of the Americas was liquidated by the Royal Bank of Canada during 1925. The Royal Bank of Canada is a very strong and well known Canadian institution and possessed at the end of 1924 some 656 branches of which 111 were in foreign countries.[29]

The American Express Company, Inc.—The American Express Company was created in 1841 as a partnership enterprise to engage in express and travel business, and it established some foreign branches before 1900, the first being opened at Paris in 1895. A concern which is simply an express company is not considered to be a bank by American courts even though it may transact some banking operations.[30]   But the American Express Company, Inc., is not the American Express Company. It is a separate corporation, organized by the American Express Company on February 20, 1919 under the laws of the State of Connecticut with a capital of $6,000,000 for the purpose of taking over the foreign branches of the company.

By 1921 the thirty-eight foreign branches owned by the American Express Company had been transferred to the American Express Company, Inc.[31]   On June 30, 1926 the corporation had forty-seven foreign branches which were distributed as follows: Argentina, one; Belgium, three; Ceylon, one; China, four; Denmark, one; Egypt, one; France, five; Germany, three; Great Britain, eight; Greece, two; Holland, two; India, two; Italy, four; Japan, one; Monaco, one; Palestine, one; Philippine Islands, one; Straits Settlements, one; Switzerland, three; Turkey, two. A number of these foreign offices are operated by subsidiary corporations organized under the laws of the foreign countries where they are situated.[32]

---

[29] The statement of condition on November 29, 1924 shows: paid-in capital $20,400,000; reserves $20,400,000; undivided profits $1,143,806; deposits $461,836,583; total assets $583,789,509. At the end of 1925 the bank had over 900 branches, all except about 100 being located in Canada.

[30] Wells v. Northern Pacific Railroad Company, 23 Fed. 469, 471, 10 Sawy. 441.

[31] Condition on December 31, 1925: capital $6,000,000; surplus and undivided profits $977,611; deposits $15,359,311; total resources $33,018,768.

[32] For example, The American Express Company, S.A.I., Italy; the American Express Company, G.M.B.H., Germany; the American Express Company, A.S., Denmark; the American Express Company, A.B., Sweden; the American Express Company,

The charter of the corporation divides its operations into three main divisions, authorizing it to engage in the express and freight forwarding business, to carry on the operations of a travel agency, and to exercise all the powers of a foreign banking corporation. The mere fact that the corporation is not specifically limited to banking operations would not preclude its classification as a banking institution. The well-known International Banking Corporation, for example, is empowered by its charter to engage in practically any business under the sun. In the case of such corporations it is the trend of their activities, rather than the provisions of their charters, which must determine whether they shall be eventually classified as banking institutions. The American Express Company, Inc., has been increasingly engaging in banking operations. It is regarded as a bank in foreign countries, and is listed as one of the "foreign banks which have been authorized to maintain agencies in New York State" by the Superintendent of Banks of the State of New York. Such a corporation can hardly be left out of consideration in a study of American branch banks abroad.

Summary

Foreign Branch Banking Expansion by American Commercial Banks.—What judgment shall be passed upon the foreign expansion of American banks; what success has been met with in the establishment of branch banks abroad? The expansion of the first group of banking institutions, the national banks and state trust companies, through the establishment of direct foreign branches must be regarded as quite successful. Eleven banking institutions are included in this group. Taking the whole period 1887 to 1926 we find that only one of all the regular foreign branches established or acquired by ten

A.S., Norway. The subsidiary method was used to evade laws prohibiting the establishment of branches by foreign corporations or placing branches of such corporations at a disadvantage. The reasons which made the use of the subsidiary advisable in Italy and Germany no longer exist but subsidiaries are still necessary in Norway and Sweden.

of these institutions has been closed. The other bank opened a very large number of branches in a too rapid expansion and subsequently withdrew a quarter of them.

Three of the eleven banks no longer figure in foreign branch banking but the branches they opened are still in operation as offices of other American banks. The Jarvis-Conklin Mortgage Trust Company and the North American Trust Company (later named the Trust Company of America) went out of business but the foreign branch established by the first bank and subsequently transferred to the second is now one of the Equitable Trust Company's branches. The Commercial National Bank of Washington, D. C., sold its two foreign branches in 1918, but the branches are still functioning under the present ownership of the Chase National Bank after having passed through the ownership of the American Foreign Banking Corporation.

All the regular branches, except one, established by seven other domestic banks are still in operation. The one referred to was the Constantinople branch of the Guaranty Trust Company, opened in 1920 and closed in 1922. The Guaranty Trust Company established eight other regular branches which are still being maintained and a war emergency office at London and one at Tours which were withdrawn after the need for them ceased to exist. The Farmers' Loan and Trust Company opened two regular foreign branches. One of these was bought, and is now operated, by the National City Bank of New York. The other is still owned by the Farmers' Loan and Trust Company. The company installed three special agencies in France for the convenience of American troops during the war, and these were closed after the armistice. The Equitable Trust Company established three regular foreign branches; the Bankers Trust Company, two; the First National Bank of Boston, two; the Empire Trust Company, one; and the Chase National Bank acquired three. All of these branches are still in operation.

Successful Foreign Expansion.—In all, these ten banking institutions established twenty-two regular foreign branch banks and acquired one branch installed by a foreign banking corporation—the Havana City branch of the American Foreign Banking Corporation which was taken over by the Chase National Bank in 1925. Twenty-two of these twenty-three regular foreign branches were never closed and continue in active operation today. The only other direct foreign offices opened by these banks were the five emergency offices mentioned. These were all installed in England and France to aid in the prosecution of the World War and were withdrawn when their services were no longer needed by the American forces in Europe.

The remaining American bank interested in direct foreign branches is the National City Bank of New York. It did not start its foreign expansion until after the outbreak of the World War, being prevented from doing so until the establishment of the Federal Reserve System late in 1914. The bank established in all sixty-four foreign branches of which seventeen were withdrawn. The reasons for the withdrawal of these branches are essentially the same as those applying to the war-born foreign banking corporations.

The Foreign Expansion of Foreign Trade Banks.—The foreign expansion of the American foreign banking corporations, other than the two which are the subsidiaries of two great American commercial banks, ended in complete failure. These foreign banking corporations or foreign trade banks established in all, at one time or another, eighty-one foreign branches, and acquired two.[33] Only one of the branches originally established by the foreign trade banks remains in operation as a branch of an American bank—the present Havana City branch of the Chase National Bank.

---

[33] Not counting the 23 offices tranferred upon the reorganization of the Mercantile Bank of the Americas into the Bank of Central and South America.

Reasons for Failures.—The foreign expansion of these corporations was disastrous, and that of the National City Bank was not wholly successful because of two main reasons: the expansion was unduly rapid and unwarranted; trained men for the management of foreign branch banks were lacking.

Success in the field of overseas banking requires a special managerial capacity which can only be developed by long years of training in actual foreign branch banking practice. Capable branch bank managers and experienced staffs cannot be made in a day. The United States had no such men, and, although some of our institutions endeavored to produce them by intensive training schools, it was found that they could not be manufactured on short notice. The development of able branch bank personnel is a matter of time and patience. The extraordinary success of the British and Canadian banks in foreign branch banking indicates the value of long training for the men who are to represent their banks in foreign fields. The future branch manager of a British or Canadian bank has entered into the employ of the bank by his eighteenth birthday. He remains there for several years until he has been thoroughly trained in banking practice and in the policies of the bank. After this period of preparation he goes to a foreign branch having an old and experienced staff and his training is continued. When he finally rises to the position of manager he may be regarded as fully adequate to the demands of the position. It is by this long drawn out method that British and Canadian banks have built up the personnel of their foreign branches, and there seems to be no shorter road to real success in overseas banking. The failure of many of the American foreign branch banks established during the war period was due, to a great extent, to untrained and inexperienced management.

Not all the blame is to be placed upon the branch managers. The home offices, carried away by the business optimism which grew steadily from 1914 to 1920, saw everywhere what they thought to be excellent opportunities for profitable branch bank operation. The rising prices caused by the abnormal war demands gave a great impetus to trade and American and other foreign branch banks were established in large numbers in Cuba, South America, and the Orient. But the abnormal demand fell off in 1920 and many of our branches were found to be in towns of normally little or no commercial importance. In such cases withdrawal of branches was inevitable no matter how capable the managers. Very generally, however, the managers showed a lack of conservatism and sound policy. In many cases branches embarked on policies of ruinous competition with native banks and branches of foreign banks. They lowered rates, incurring the antagonism of native institutions, and granted credit upon anything but sound bases. The policies of branch banks in Cuba were typical.

In the case of Cuba, funds were advanced on sugar held in storage in the warehouses of the seaports at rates which barely left a margin of 10 per cent of the prevailing inflated price for sugar. Not only that, but on a similar basis advances were made against prospective crops and also on plantations and centrals; the result being that after a period when profits were reaped in the greatest abundance and increasing impetus was given to further expansion, another era had to take place to bring things back to natural and normal conditions.

Prices of commodities responded to the decreased demand for all staples. New market prices could not cover the amounts advanced on goods in storage. Branches of banks, using all resources available, were compelled to place a lien on whatever securities could be obtained from their creditors to further guarantee loans, which in several cases were covered by staples already considerably depreciated in value and in some cases totally unsalable. Such is the reason why even lands, plantations and buildings were placed in the hands of the banks by creditors who a few months before had considered their affairs in prosperous and healthy circumstances and now found themselves practically bankrupt. In many cases planters and merchants (the borrowers) were not totally responsible for their new financial condition. Their financiers did not find it convenient to give them advice: a silent advice through credit curtailment, that unreasonable expansion was not at all expedient in spite of the booming situation at the time.[34]

Real Progress Made.—The foreign expansion of American banks in the war and post-war periods presents some pages which make sorry reading, but it is not necessary to view the future of American foreign branch banking with misgivings. It happened that certain institutions expanded too rapidly in an abnormal period and the over-extended equipment of these establishments had to be reduced when conditions returned to normal. A great number of banking offices were opened abroad and many were closed, but a great deal of real progress was made. In 1913 there were only six foreign branches of four American commercial banks and twenty branches of two American foreign banking corporations. In 1926 there were one hundred and seven foreign branches of eight American commercial banks. Seventy-two were direct branches and thirty-five were foreign offices of the subsidiaries of two of the banks. This expansion of over 400 per cent appears to be permanent. Since 1925 no withdrawals have occurred and the movement has been toward slow expansion in the number of American branch banks abroad.

---

[34] G. B. Sherwell, *Journal* of American Bankers Association, October, 1922, p. 206.

CHAPTER X

THE FOREIGN BRANCHES OF FEDERAL RESERVE BANKS AND THE DEVELOPMENT OF AMERICAN BANK ACCEPTANCES

The establishment of foreign branches by the federal reserve banks and the development of American bankers' acceptances are subjects of interest in the study of American foreign banking expansion and will be given some mention at this point.

Branches of the Federal Reserve Banks

The federal reserve banks, which were authorized by the Federal Reserve Act to establish branches at home and abroad, have located twenty-three branches in the United States. The first was installed at New Orleans, Louisiana, in 1915, five were established in 1917, ten in 1918, four in 1919, two in 1920, and one in 1921 at Helena, Montana.

Question of Foreign Branches.—It was thought at first by some that the federal reserve banks would establish branches abroad, breaking the way for branches of our commercial banks and supporting the losses of pioneering. Such a policy had its appeal to many bankers but others looked upon any extension of federal reserve bank branches abroad as dangerous competition for the foreign offices of American commercial banks.

Secretary of the Treasury McAdoo in his report to the President, September 6, 1915, believed that the federal reserve banks should take the initiative in entering the foreign field,—"The federal reserve banks could, with the consent of the Federal Reserve Board, establish joint agencies in each of the countries of Latin America." The report stressed the need of a powerful consolidated banking organization for foreign trade such as only the twelve reserve banks could create. The Secretary judged the resources of our own individual banks insufficient for the task, whereas "The combined capital stock and resources of our federal reserve banks utilized in this way for the extension and promotion of our foreign commerce would give them unrivaled financial power. They could maintain themselves in the foreign fields in competition with the world and perform a service of incalculable value to the American people."

The Federal Reserve Board, after discussing the question, decided that since the federal reserve banks were "bankers' banks," holding the reserves of all member banks in the Federal Reserve System, they could not be allowed to do pioneering in foreign markets. It was held that the granting of credit facilities by foreign branches of federal reserve banks would lead to a lock-up of reserve money in loans which in most cases would be subject to wide fluctuations of exchange. As depositaries of the reserves of member banks, the reserve banks are restricted to certain operations in order that their funds may be always kept highly liquid, and thus are not as qualified to meet the competition of foreign banks in overseas markets as are our commercial banks. In refusing to permit the establishment of foreign branches by federal reserve banks, the Board stated its willingness to aid American foreign branch banks by favoring American bank acceptances and by appointing foreign correspondents for this purpose where it might be judged necessary.

Federal Reserve Bank Branches in Cuba.—There have been but two branches of federal reserve banks established outside the territory of the United States, and these are both in Cuba at Havana. United States currency is legal tender in

Cuba and a considerable portion of this currency in circulation on the island consists of federal reserve notes of the Federal Reserve Bank of Atlanta, Georgia. This bank petitioned the Federal Reserve Board to be allowed to establish a branch in Cuba, fearing that if another federal reserve bank installed a branch its notes would be retired from circulation by the latter. At this time the Federal Reserve Bank of Boston also wished to locate a branch in Cuba and was willing to maintain the circulation of the federal reserve notes of the Atlanta bank. So on June 28, 1923 the Federal Reserve Board authorized the two banks to establish agencies in Havana. By the terms of the authorization, the Havana branch of the Federal Reserve Bank of Atlanta is restricted to current operations and may buy and sell bills of exchange, drafts, etc., only upon request of the branch of the Federal Reserve Bank of Boston,— except in the case of bills drawn on drawees in the Sixth Federal Reserve District.[1] On the other hand, the Havana branch of the Federal Reserve Bank of Boston is authorized to buy and sell drafts, bills, etc., and to engage generally in the operations of a federal reserve bank except that it may not pay out its own federal reserve notes in Cuba unless in case of an insufficient supply of the currency of the Federal Reserve Bank of Atlanta the latter bank so requests.

The federal reserve bank branches in Cuba act as agencies for the withdrawal of unfit United States currency from circulation and for its replacement by new bills, and they also tend to stabilize banking conditions on the island. The commercial banks operating in Cuba are enabled to carry on their business without the necessity of holding abnormal reserves and are able to obtain currency at any time by selling bills of exchange arising out of import and export operations.

Correspondent Relations With Foreign Central Banks.— In the dealings of the Federal Reserve System with the central

---

[1] This is the district of the Federal Reserve Bank of Atlanta.

banks of foreign nations the immediate operating relations and the correspondence are conducted by the Federal Reserve Bank of New York which represents all the federal reserve banks. The other reserve banks participate ratably in the system's foreign operations which are under the general supervision of the Federal Reserve Board. The Federal Reserve Bank of New York established correspondent relationships with some of the foreign central banks in 1916 and since that year other foreign banks of issue have been added to the list of foreign correspondents of the system. In the early years the transactions with the foreign correspondents related for the most part to the war, to the reparations commission and to reconstruction, but during the past two years the most important transactions have been in connection with the programs adopted by various foreign countries in the reestablishment of gold as the basis of their monetary systems. In this connection loans secured by gold were made by the Federal Reserve Bank of New York, with participation of the other reserve banks, to the Bank of Poland, to the banking office of the ministry of finance of Czechoslovakia and to the Bank of England, and arrangements were made to buy prime commercial bills from the Bank of Belgium, when and if desired.[2]

The central banks of many foreign countries hold funds on deposit in the Federal Reserve Bank of New York and from time to time instruct the bank to invest these funds in acceptances in the New York market. Bills held by the bank on account of such foreign correspondents were $65,000,000 at the end of 1925 as compared with $43,000,000 at the close of 1924 and $19,000,000 at the end of 1923.[3]

Opposition to Foreign Branches of Reserve Banks.— Other than the agencies in Cuba of the federal reserve banks, there are no federal reserve bank offices outside the territory

---

[2] Annual Report of the Federal Reserve Board, 1925, pp. 10–14.
[3] *Ibid.*, p. 11.

of the United States, and no further expansion is at present contemplated. Even the establishment of the reserve bank agencies in Cuba called forth a protest from the American Bankers Association which condemned "the opening of such branches in Cuba specifically." [4] The competition of federal reserve bank branches in foreign markets is quite feared by most American commercial bankers, and since the Federal Reserve Board is not in favor of foreign expansion due to the peculiar character of the federal reserve banks, it is not likely that foreign branches of these banks will be established abroad in the near future.

Development of American Bank Acceptances

Sterling and Dollar Exchange.—Had it not been for the war the development of American bank acceptances would have been extremely slow and difficult. Before 1914 American bank acceptances were not yet in existence and merchants all over the world were accustomed to buy and sell their wares in foreign trade on the basis of sterling which had become an international money. But the great war and post-war trade found New York to be the only market with an adequate supply of credits. Moreover, sterling fluctuated so much in 1915 that it became an unsatisfactory medium for future payments, and although it was pegged at about $4.76 from January, 1916 to March, 1919 by the use of $1,400,000,000 in conscripted American and Canadian securities, gold shipments, import restrictions, and credits obtained from the United States, this artificial stabilization did not restore full confidence in sterling exchange. When pegging ceased in March, 1919 sterling began an abrupt decline until it reached a record low of $3.19 for cables and $3.18 for demand in February, 1920. Since that date sterling tended upward but did not touch par until February 3, 1926.[5] The

[4] *Commerce and Finance*, 1923, p. 1825.
[5] *Wall Street Journal*, February 3, 1926.

dollar meanwhile was relatively stable and New York rates were lower than London's except for a short period at the beginning of the war. All these conditions created by the war aided the development of the market for dollar exchange.

Slow Development.—In the United States, our bank (or bankers) acceptances have had to compete with the call loan, commercial paper and bond markets. The government's war-financing operations in connection with marketing its bonds cut down the market for acceptances for several years. American bankers were accustomed to invest their surplus funds in the call loan market and they could not be expected suddenly to change the character of their investments, even though acceptances were made as attractive in yield and liquidity as call loans. American business men engaged in foreign trade had to learn the advantage of changing from the use of foreign acceptance credits to American bank acceptances. During the early days of the American bank acceptance, Paul M. Warburg, speaking before the New York State Bankers Association, declared:

It is a strange fact that many of our business men who enjoy the reputation of being keen and progressive are actually wasting their funds by still using foreign acceptance credits instead of American.

At Rio de Janeiro I found to my surprise that the majority of American coffee importers were still using letters of credit in sterling for which they were paying a discount rate of 4¾%, as against the American discount rate of 2%.

Moreover, in so doing, they were often paying two commissions, one to the foreign banker, who issues, and one to the American banker who opens the credit, instead of paying a single commission to the American banker.

There is always such inertia to be broken down when changing from one method to another in the business world. But some of the commercial banks at New York and the federal reserve banks began early vigorously to employ their efforts to create a market for American bank acceptances, and the progress made up to the entry of the United States into the war was as satisfactory as could have been expected. The Guaranty Trust Company of New York was the pioneer among the former in this work. It started in immediately to use dollar letters of credit, but when foreign bills drawn under them were first offered, the company had to bid for them itself. Soon other banks and brokers began to bid, and the movement got under way. Gradually, investors of every conceivable kind wishing to employ their idle funds over short periods came into the market for bank acceptances, broadening it and swelling the demand coming from banking institutions.

Support of Bankers' Acceptances by Federal Reserve System.—The policy of the Federal Reserve Board in regard to bank acceptances was to bring them into use gradually in order to avoid the dangers and abuses which would arise from a sudden introduction.[6] The Board deemed the establishment of a discount market essential for the financing of American foreign trade by American banks, for the exercise of credit control by the federal reserve banks, and for the equalization of interest rates in the money markets of the world. Since the discount market in foreign countries is based upon the bank acceptance the federal reserve banks endeavored to build up a discount market in the United States "by encouraging the use of bankers' acceptances and by freely dealing in them."[7] The report of the Federal Reserve Board for 1916 stated: "The Board notes with great satisfaction the progress made during the past year in developing a market for American bankers' acceptances which now enjoy the standing to which they are entitled in most of the world's financial centers. . . . A very satisfactory beginning has been made, but it should be borne in mind that it is only a beginning."[8]

---

[6] See H. L. Reed, *op. cit.*, pp. 160–170; and H. P. Willis, Federal Reserve System, pp. 996–1007, on abuses of bank acceptances.
[7] Tenth annual report of the Federal Reserve Board, 1924, p. 12.
[8] Report of the Federal Reserve Board, 1916, p. 4.

Rise to Importance of American Bank Acceptances.— Since 1915 when American banks began accepting generally the market for American bankers' acceptances under the encouragement of the Federal Reserve System has grown to a position of substantially equal importance with the commercial paper market, and the bankers' acceptance has taken a place of considerable importance in financing our foreign trade where over more than half the transactions are financed by American bank acceptances.

The American bank acceptance, non-existent before 1914, has become favorably known all over the world. The business of granting such credits has come to concentrate in the hands of some seventy-five American banking institutions, the most important of which are in the city of New York.[9] On January 30, 1926, American banks had acceptances outstanding to the amount of $788,253,933, and American bank acceptances were being used to finance an average of over $3,500,000,000 of business yearly, the greater part of which related to the financing of exports and imports. Before the World War, practically all of the financing of American foreign trade was done through London and other foreign centers.

Appearance of Acceptance Houses.—Nearly all the leading American banks, trust companies and private banking institutions now do an acceptance business and a number of purely acceptance houses have appeared. The largest of these houses are the International Acceptance Bank, the Kidder, Peabody Acceptance Corporation, the J. Henry Schroeder Banking Corporation, and the French-American Banking Corporation. Paul M. Warburg, chairman of the first-mentioned bank stated in his annual report for 1925 that the bank's acceptances outstanding on December 31 of that year were drawn by 409 drawers in 25 foreign countries and covered transactions in-

---

[9] By 1926 some 200 banks were handling practically all the acceptance business (as against about 500 banks in 1919) while 75 of these banks were doing approximately 90 per cent of the business.

volving all the important raw commodities in world trade. Of the bank's total $46,527,794 acceptance credits outstanding, $18,487,900 covered exports from the United States, $15,440,-874 imports, and $10,559,141 movement of merchandise between foreign countries.

Branch Banks and Bank Acceptances.—American bankers' acceptances may be used to finance our own foreign commerce and also the trade between other countries. At present we are largely financing our own imports as well as large amounts of our exports, and we are sharing with London and other foreign financial centers in the financing of the movement of goods between foreign countries.[10] The development of New York as a foreign trade financing center depends upon its maintenance of a discount market capable of absorbing great amounts of bills at rates running as low as those of foreign money markets. No small part of the support of American bank acceptances comes from the making of American foreign investments and the buying and selling of bills on New York by the foreign branches of American banks. The movement of American funds abroad and the increase in our foreign commerce are being reflected in the steady growth of the volume of American bank acceptances.

---

[10] Classification of American bank acceptances on March 31, 1926: imports $333,-773,008; exports $257,414,457; movement of goods between foreign countries $37,-899,986; domestic $19,175,584; warehoused credits $80,499,897; dollar exchange $16,896,700.

CHAPTER XI

THE LEGAL STATUS OF AMERICAN BRANCH BANKS IN THE PRINCIPAL COUNTRIES

In any serious study of the American branch banks abroad it is necessary to inquire into their legal status in the foreign countries where they operate to ascertain whether or not they are hampered in their installation and operation by laws favoring the native banks. Such an examination will also enable Americans to appreciate the importance of the restrictions which our laws impose on foreign banks wishing to establish and operate branches in this country.

France

Rights of American Banks in France.—A bank authorized by American laws to establish foreign branches and engage in foreign operations may open and operate branches in France without any special authorization of the French Government.[1] The decree of the French Government promulgated August 6, 1882 declares that American corporations may exercise all their rights and appear in court in conforming to the laws of France. The expression "all their rights" means all the rights recognized as belonging to French corporations [2] and all the rights which could be exercised by individuals of American nation-

---

[1] The decree of August 6, 1882 promulgated by virtue of the law of May 30, 1857 extended to the United States the benefits of Article 1 of this law which provided that: "Corporations and other commercial, industrial or financial associations which are at their creation subject to the authorization of the Belgian Government and which have obtained it are allowed to exercise all their rights and appear in the courts of justice in France, provided they conform to the laws of the Empire." Article 2 of the law stated that "An imperial decree . . . may apply the benefits of Article 1 to other countries."

[2] Barazzetti, *op. cit.*, p. 79.

ality.[3] An American bank or any other American corporation may sue and be sued in France just as if it were a French corporation or individual, but it must furnish, if requested, a special bail or security called "cautio judicatum solvi" in order to assure payment of the expenses.[4] This security is generally required.

All questions arising as to the regularity of the constitution of the bank, its mode of designation, its functioning, the powers and responsibility of its managers, the causes of dissolution, and the validity of changes made in its by-laws are decided by its own national laws provided that no conditions contrary to French laws of public order arise.[5] All foreign banks are admitted to the exchange and to the clearing house, and may also become members of the Association des Banques et Banquiers as well as the Union Syndicale des Banquiers. The Bank of France receives the bills for discount and the acceptances offered by foreign banks on the same basis as those presented by French banks. The American and other foreign banks in France possess, in short, all the rights accorded to French banking establishments.

Formalities to be Observed.—Certain formalities, however, must be performed by every bank or other corporation before operating in France, and others must be complied with during operation. These formalities are required by the public interest, and are as follows:

INSTALLATION.—There are two sets of formalities to be fulfilled by corporations for the installation of a business in France. The one is for the purpose of furnishing information to the government upon the nature of the concern; the other is to assure the payment of the taxes and any fines which the establishment may have to discharge. Both sets of formalities

---

[3] C. G. Loeb, Legal Status of American Corporations in France, p. 57.

[4] Article 16 of the Code Civil modified by the law of March 5, 1895.

[5] Société des Glacières Boulonnaises v. Evans, Cour de Cassation, December 26, 1905. A supreme court decision to be found in Clunet's *Journal du Droit International Privé*, 1906, p. 449.

must be executed in due form or the corporation will be exposed to a fine or closure.[6]   The fiscal formalities, which must be discharged before opening for business, are the following:

1. The bank must furnish to the Direction Générale de l'Enregistrement des Domaines et du Timbre certified copies of its constitution and by-laws.   These documents must be authenticated by a French consul in the United States.[7]

2. The bank must sign an engagement relative to the payment of taxes and any fines which may be imposed, and further, must either appoint a representative of French nationality to be responsible for the payment of the taxes and fines [8] or deposit a security in currency.[9]

In order to satisfy the second set of formalities which are for the purpose of giving information to the government concerning the nature of the corporation, the bank must register at the Tribunal de Commerce within one month after its opening in France.   At this registration the bank must furnish a statement containing the information required by Article 6 of the law of March 18, 1919: its name, capital, object, duration of charter, location of all its branches in France and elsewhere, names and nationality of its members, and other information of the same nature.

OPERATION.—During its operation in France the American branch bank is subject to all French laws of public order. It is governed by the same regulations as apply to French banks in all that concerns banking, and may be declared bankrupt by the French courts.[10]   It pays the same taxes as those imposed upon

---

[6] C. G. Loeb, *op. cit.*, pp. 133, 194, 195.
[7] Article 12 of the law of April 13, 1898.
[8] Article 3 of the Decree of December 6, 1874.
[9] Article 12 of the law of April 13, 1898: Decree of June 22, 1898, Art. 1.
[10] Houpin et Bosvieux, Traité Générale des Sociétés, Vol. III, p. 157. See also the case Philippe, Berkowitz v. Banque Impériale Ottomane, Tribunal de Commerce de la Seine, May 14, 1906, Clunet 1906, p. 1143.

French banks but in discharging one of these taxes which is called "centimes additionels à la patente" the great capital of American banks works to their disadvantage for the tax is imposed upon the entire capital of corporations operating in France.

Here it is at a disadvantage compared with French banks. Even though they are taxed upon their entire capital, let us note that generally all this capital is employed in France, while American banks employ only a very small part of their total capital in the French market.

An American bank which has bought the branch of another bank in Paris employs the same number of people and makes the same operations, but it pays a "patente" triple that paid by the preceding bank because of the great size of its capital, even though the capital it employs in France is no larger. This tax is generally heavier than the other taxes and can be hampering for the American banks which have larger capitalizations than the French banks. For example, the National City Bank of New York pays the tax on its entire capital of about $100,000,000 but it has only one branch in France; the Société Générale (one of the great French Banks) pays this tax also on its entire capital of 500,000,000 francs (about $100,000,000 at par) but this capital represents 603 branches, 27 agencies and 600 seasonal offices in France.[11]

This tax, however, was not framed with any intention in mind on the part of the French Government to place foreign banks in a position of disadvantage, and it may be easily evaded by changing an American branch bank into a "French" corporation or by creating a subsidiary bank with a small capital in the United States to establish branches in France. It is interesting to note in this connection that the Paris branch of the National City Bank of New York was reorganized into a French corporation (société anonyme) on May 18, 1924.

At the end of each fiscal year every bank or other commercial enterprise in France must send a balance sheet which includes its operations in France and elsewhere to the Enregistre-

---

[11] C. W. Phelps, Banques Américaines à l'Etranger et principalement en France, pp. 106–7.

ment,[12] and must also open its books to the agents of the Enregistrement for examination in order to determine the taxes to
be paid.[13] The American branch bank like all other corporations operating in France, must have printed upon its letterheads and all other papers sent to the public the number assigned to it in the Commercial Register.[14]

Such is the legal situation of American branch banks in
France.[15] Our establishments in that country enjoy the same
rights and are submitted to the same obligations as the
French establishments.

England

Liberal Viewpoint of British.—The policy of England has
always been to encourage foreign traders and business men to
do as much business with Great Britain as possible, and one of
the fundamental principles of this commercial policy has been
to allow foreign merchants complete liberty in their operations
in the United Kingdom. The presence of foreign banks in
London is a benefit in that it tends to enlarge the basis of the
financial market, multiply the points of banking contact with
the rest of the world, and augment the prestige of the London
money market. In view of the importance of London as a
financial center it is not difficult to appreciate the English Government's liberal policy in welcoming the establishment of foreign banks in the British metropolis.

English bankers support this liberal viewpoint for they
are so firmly established in their home market that they have
nothing whatever to fear from the competition of foreign
banks in England and they have everything to gain. They
energetically demand a policy of international reciprocity; that

---

[12] Banque Impériale des Pays Autrichiens v. l'Enregistrement, Cour de Cassation (Req), June 19, 1908. This supreme court case is in Clunet 1909, p. 1094.

[13] Veyrièras, Sociétés Étrangères en France, pp. 145–46.

[14] Article 1 of the law of June 1, 1923, in effect December 5, 1923.

[15] The situation of foreign branch banks is similar in Belgium, except that they
may not discount bills at the National Bank unless Belgian banks enjoy corresponding rights in the home countries of the foreign branch banks.

is, they wish their own foreign branches to enjoy the same equality of treatment in foreign countries as that accorded to the branches of foreign banks in British territory. To bring about such a condition of reciprocity, the National British Committee reporting to the International Chamber of Commerce in 1921 was of the opinion that pressure should be brought to bear on those countries which impose restrictions upon foreign banks in order that inequalities of treatment disappear,—at least for the banks of the countries not imposing restrictions.[16]

Formalities.—There are but few formalities to be complied with in opening and operating a foreign branch bank in the United Kingdom.

INSTALLATION.—The dispositions governing foreign corporations in the United Kingdom are to be found in Article 274 of the Companies Act of 1908. Article 274 requires certain information to be furnished by foreign corporations, banks therein included. Every corporation organized outside the United Kingdom must, within one month after opening a place of business in the United Kingdom, furnish to the Registrar of Companies:

1. A certified copy of its constitution, by-laws and statutes.
2. A list of its directors and other persons exercising the functions of directors whatever may be their designation.
3. The names and addresses of one or several persons residing in the United Kingdom authorized to receive in the name of the corporation all legal notices sent it.

OPERATION.—During its period of operation in the United Kingdom, a foreign corporation is not called upon to discharge any particular obligation not required of native institutions.

---

[16] Traitement des Banques Étrangères, p. 16.

It pays taxes upon the same basis as the domestic concerns, and must deposit with the Registrar of Companies each year a statement of condition the same as do the native banks. The Registrar must also be notified of any changes which occur in the documents submitted at the time of installation.

If the foreign corporation establishing a branch in the United Kingdom employ the word "Limited" in its name, it must, in addition to the preceding, indicate the country in which it was organized in all notices and circulars soliciting subscriptions for its shares or debentures in the United Kingdom, post visibly in all places of business in Great Britain its name and country of origin, and indicate the same facts on all letterheads, notices, advertisements, etc.

Disadvantages.—The various formalities and obligations imposed on foreign banks in the United Kingdom expose the establishments to fines or closure in case of non-performance. The rights and obligations of foreign branch banks in the United Kingdom are essentially the same as those of the domestic institutions. Nevertheless, a mention must be made of two points in conclusion. Foreign banks are not admitted to the London clearing house. This is a disadvantage but foreign banks are not the only ones to suffer since only a small number of British banks are admitted: those which have created and maintained the clearing house. Another disadvantage experienced by foreign banks arises from the Bank of England's policy of discounting for native banks at a preferential rate and not buying the acceptances of foreign banks domiciled in London or of foreign branch banks in that center. Such acceptances, however, can be sold in the London market at rates that are little, if at all, discriminatory.

Italy

Freedom to Install and Operate.—Italy has always been liberal in her treatment of foreigners. Citizens of other coun-

tries living in Italy and foreigners setting up an establishment
or a branch in Italian territory have the same rights and are
governed by the same regulations as Italian individuals and corporations.   However, due to the attitude of several countries
toward Italian citizens and enterprises the Italian Government
was led to pass legislation which may be used to restrict foreign
banks in their operations in Italy.

The dispositions which apply to foreign banking institutions
transacting business in Italian territory are found in the Decree No. 1620 of September 4, 1919 and in Articles 230–232 of
the Commercial Code.

INSTALLATION.—In order to establish a branch in Italy the
foreign bank must first procure an authorization from the
Minister of the Treasury.   The petition must be accompanied
by a certified copy of the constitution and by-laws of the bank
and a statement giving: the amount of capital to be devoted to
operations in Italy, names and addresses of directors and managers of the parent bank and branches, location of home office,
object, and information of like nature.

In granting the authorization a registry fee proportional to
the amount of capital to be employed in Italy is imposed,[17] and
the authorization may only be accorded by the Minister of the
Treasury with the agreement of the Minister of Foreign Affairs and the Minister of Industry, Commerce and Labor.   Furthermore, Article 2 of the Decree No. 1620 provides that the
Minister of the Treasury shall not make his decision until after
having examined the treatment accorded to Italian corporations by the country to which the petitioning bank belongs.   The
Minister of the Treasury may restrict the operations in Italy
of a foreign corporation or he may refuse to authorize it to
operate in the country.   His decision is final.

OPERATION.—Within three months after the reception of
an authorization to do business in Italy, the foreign bank must
fulfill the formalities set forth in Articles 230, 231 and 232 of

---

[17] Decree No. 2163, November 24, 1919.

the Commercial Code which call for registration at the Commercial Registry of the bank's charter and full information upon its nature and operations. Any later change must be forthwith communicated to the Minister of the Treasury.

The foreign branch bank in Italy must publish a separate balance sheet showing the operations of the bank in Italian territory in accordance with Article 4 of the Decree No. 1620. During operation it is required to publish during the first week of each month a statement of condition for the past month. It pays taxes upon the same basis as the native banks.

Foreign branch banks in Italy may become members of the clearing house, and in general have every right possessed by Italian establishments. Even though the government has power to restrict or prohibit foreign banks through Article 2 of the Decree No. 1620, no restrictions whatever have been imposed upon the activities of foreign banks in Italy, not even in the case of the branch banks of the United States where the operations of foreign branches are severely restricted.

Spain

Trend Toward Restriction.—In late years there has been an increasing tendency in Spain in the direction of favoring national industry and commerce at the expense of foreigners. The law of March 2, 1917 passed with the object of favoring the creation of new industries in Spain and the development of those existing, accorded numerous favors to the native concerns at the expense of foreign establishments. The law of October 19, 1920 provided for special taxes on foreign banks. Dispositions 7 and 8 of the law established a tax on every company which should amount to not less than 6 per cent of the profits or to not less than three per thousand on the capital. Disposition 9 subjected to this tax:

A. Every Spanish or foreign enterprise which operates exclusively in the Kingdom, for the total amount of its profits or capital.

B. Every foreign enterprise which operates both in Spain and without, for that part of its profits or capital corresponding to the business of the enterprise in the Kingdom. In no case may this part be less than one-tenth of the entire capital of the company.

Disposition 11 declares:

Notwithstanding that which has been said in the preceding Disposition, paragraph B, the minimum tax on the capital of foreign banks established in Spain shall be determined in the following fashion: (a) one per thousand on the total capital of the establishment, (b) two per thousand on the part of the capital employed in Spain, established in the manner indicated above.[18]

The taxation of the entire capital of a bank having a branch in Spain made the branch bank method disadvantageous as a means of foreign banking expansion into that country, and foreign banks of large capitalization sought to evade this taxation. The National City Bank of New York, for example, transferred its branches at Madrid and Barcelona to the International Banking Corporation, its subsidiary, a few months after the tax law was passed. The capital of the corporation amounts to only about one-tenth of the capital of the bank. Thus the tax on the total capital and the tax on that part of the capital employed in Spain amount to very much less for the branches as offices of the International Banking Corporation than it would be if they were direct offices of the bank.

Further in regard to taxation, Article 3 of the law of December 29, 1910 authorizes the Government to surtax foreign establishments in Spain whose countries of origin tax Spanish concerns unfavorably. Article 28 of the Decree of April 25, 1911 declares that a Spanish establishment abroad which has to pay a tax superior to those paid by foreign firms of the same kind in Spain should notify the Spanish Treasury and that the Treasury should raise the tax on the foreign companies concerned in Spain to an equivalence.

---

[18] That is to say that the part of the capital taxed as being employed in Spain will in no case be estimated to be less than one-tenth of the total capital of the bank. This tax is in addition to the tax on the total capital of the bank.

Rights and Formalities.—The rights, the formalities of establishment and the obligations to which foreign banks are submitted during their period of activity in Spain are largely similar to those obtaining in France and Italy—with this notation that the Bank of Spain discounts for native banks at a rate 1 per cent lower than for foreign establishments. The law relative to foreign banking in Spain is, as yet, seemingly unsettled and may very possibly become more restrictive.

Brazil

Closer Regulation of Banking.—Since the war a movement for the closer regulation of banking has grown up in Brazil and has had as a result the Decree No. 14728 of March 16, 1921 which comprehends all banking institutions in Brazil, domestic as well as foreign.[19] Up to this time banking was governed in Brazil, just as in most other countries, by the general commercial law applying to all kinds of business organizations. Corporations were regulated by the provisions of the Decree No. 434 of July 4, 1891 which required, under Article 47, that foreign corporations obtain an authorization from the government before operating in Brazil. Article 65 demanded that one-tenth of the capital of the establishment to be opened be placed, in money, in a bank of issue in Brazil or in the hands of a person under the control of the Brazilian Government, and Article 79 required the deposit of this capital, the furnishing of a copy of charter and by-laws and a list of information before opening for business in Brazil.

This legislation did not seem severe enough to the Brazilian Government and the Decree No. 14728 was promulgated in 1921. Article 4 of this decree maintains the old system of governmental authorizations. The authorization may give full

---

[19] "One fifth of the capital of Brazilian banks represents foreign capital," Dr. Correa, Chairman of the Finance Committee of the Brazilian Senate, in the *Chicago Banker*, October 17, 1925.

powers to the branches of a foreign bank or it may restrict their operations in Brazilian territory. Article 19 states that the authorization should apply the principle of reciprocity, according the foreign branch bank the same advantages and rights as those granted to Brazilian banks by the country of the former. An authorized establishment must first register with the department of bank inspection before proceeding to operate (Article 27).

INSTALLATION.—In petitioning for an authorization from the Minister of Finances, the bank must prove that it was regularly constituted under the laws of the country where it is domiciled. It must also, in conformity with Article 8 of the decree, furnish a copy of its statutes; list of stockholders with the number and value of shares held by each; statement of amount of capital to be employed in Brazil; authorization of directors to establish a branch or branches in Brazil. The bank must also agree to fulfill all the conditions imposed by the Government.

The bank is required by Article 9 to appoint a representative in Brazil fully empowered to settle all questions arising from the bank's relations with the government and with Brazilian citizens. It must agree to admit the competency of Brazilian courts for all cases in which Brazilian interests are involved. It must also engage to submit to the approbation of the Brazilian Government all changes in its statutes.

Article 20 requires that the capital of a foreign branch bank must be at least 9,000 contos of reis at the time of authorization and must never fall below this sum. Fifty per cent of the capital of the branch is to be deposited in the Brazilian Treasury or in the Bank of Brazil before it may receive its authorization to operate (Article 21).

OPERATION.—An authorized branch must begin operations, according to Article 16, within one year after the date of authorization, and must publish monthly statements of condition as provided in Article 30. At least half of the personnel of the foreign branch bank must be made up of employes of Brazilian nationality (Article 15).

If additional branches are established in Brazil, the permission of the government must be secured in each case, and the sum of 12 contos for the home office and 6 contos for every branch in Brazil must be paid annually for the expenses of bank regulation. Within two years after the date of authorization at least two-thirds of the capital destined to operations in Brazil must be paid in.

All banks transacting operations in exchange are required to deposit with the Brazilian Treasury money or Brazilian securities to an amount determined by the government in consideration of the importance of these operations (Article 34), and a list of the exchange operations made shall be delivered to the department of bank inspection daily (Article 35).

After each yearly meeting of the directors of the bank the department of bank inspection must be sent full reports of the meeting, as required by Article 31, and the yearly statement of the bank together with a list of its stockholders and the number of shares held by them is also to be sent to the department.

Protection of Brazilian Depositors.—It is interesting to note that under Article 18 the parent organization is responsible for its branches in Brazil to the effect that Brazilian creditors of the branches shall have as security not only the capital of the branches but also that of the parent institution, but, on the other hand, the statutes of the bank may not have a clause whereby the capital of the Brazilian branches may be held responsible for obligations contracted by other branches of the bank. Paragraph 1 of Article 18 also states that the failure of the foreign bank's home office or other branches shall not enable creditors to recover from the bank's branches in Brazil. Paragraph 2 gives Brazilian creditors of a failed foreign branch bank in Brazil preference over all other creditors of the branch. Thus the Brazilian Government clearly states its decision upon the important question of bankruptcy of banks doing a foreign business, a question which as yet has received no such definite treatment in the laws of most other nations.

In conclusion, it should be said that the various obligations of foreign banks in Brazil are the same as those for the native banks, and that the Brazilian constitution prohibits foreigners from being taxed at higher rates than Brazilian subjects. The importance of the recent Brazilian legislation is not that it favors Brazilian banks at the expense of foreign establishments, but that, like the legislation of the United States, it recognizes banking as a special form of business activity and regulates it strictly. The press and the foreign banking interests in Brazil voiced their disapproval of such a policy, but the Decree of 1921 was promulgated in spite of their protests.

Argentina

The Republic of Argentina has always been a very free field for foreign branch bank expansion. Legislation in this, as in most South American and other new countries, has not been developed to any such degree thus far as in the nations of Europe and in the United States.

Formalities.—Foreign corporations in Argentina are governed by the law No. 8867 of January 30, 1912. This law did away with the necessity of a governmental authorization which was previously required of foreign corporations intending to establish in Argentina. The first Article holds that the corporation must furnish a certified copy of its constitution, statutes and by-laws, and register at the Commercial Registry in Argentina. Article 2 states that the preceding Article is applicable to the corporations of countries admitting the principle of reciprocity for Argentine concerns.

During operation in Argentina the foreign branch bank is

required by Article 1 of the law No. 5125 of September 9, 1907 to send a monthly statement covering its operations in Argentina to the Government. Foreign corporations possess all the rights belonging to Argentine establishments and discharge the same obligations, including the payment of equal taxes.

Great Expansion of Foreign Banks in Argentina.— Foreign banks have taken a place of great importance in Argentina. In 1922 only eight of the thirty most important banks in the country were of Argentine nationality. The foreign banks, moreover, possessed at this time practically one-half the deposits of all banks in Argentina. It is evident that foreign banks have not encountered legal obstacles in the past in expanding into this country. Since 1920 there have been some manifestations of a tendency toward reaction against the liberty allowed foreign banking institutions. Several bills proposing to regulate more strictly or to restrict the operations of foreign banks have been introduced into the legislature but thus far none have been enacted into law. The future, however, will very probably bring stricter regulation of foreign banking establishments in Argentina.

Other Countries

Foreign Banks Treated Equally With Native Banks in Most Countries.—The preceding review of the legal situation of American foreign branch banks has been limited to those European nations in which all of the European expansion of our branch banks has taken place, and to the two South American countries in which American banking expansion has been greatest and which appear to be the largest fields for future foreign extension of American banking institutions.

In most nations, branches of foreign banks may be established and operated on a basis of equal rights and obligations

with the native banking institutions. On this basis, in addition
to the nations just studied, American banks have established
and are operating branches in Japan, China, India, Mexico,
Chile, Peru, Uruguay, Venezuela, and in the East and West
Indies. In Austria, Germany, Greece, Holland, Switzerland,
Australia, and most other countries, American banks may also
establish and operate branches upon a basis of equal treatment
with native institutions.

Prohibitions.—Finland, Poland, Norway, Sweden, Czecho-
Slovakia, and Canada prohibit the establishment of branches by
foreign banks, and the status of foreign branch banks in Russia is unsettled at present. If Canadian and Russian legislation
were made favorable to the establishment of branches by foreign banks there might be some expansion by American banks
into these countries. These two are the only countries apparently attractive to American banks that do not offer a free field
for the establishment of branch banks. In the United States,
branch bank establishment by foreign institutions is severely
restricted by the laws of the several states—indeed, it is prohibited in New York and California which are the states in
which foreign banks most desire to open and operate branches.

CHAPTER XII

THE LEGAL STATUS OF FOREIGN BANKS IN THE UNITED STATES

The Restrictive Character of American Banking Legislation

Early Banking Freedom and Abuses.—In the United States, in contrast to foreign countries in general, banking is considered to be a special form of business, demanding because of its nature a special legislation for the protection of the public. The reasons for this view are not hard to explain in the light of American banking history.

Banking in the early days of the nation was free, hardly any legislation on the subject existing. Most merchants engaged in at least some form of banking activity. Many would not only sell their customers goods on credit but would loan them money or even pay cash to a third party on the written order of a customer. Sometimes when currency was scarce, a merchant would issue his own notes to meet the demand. Banking was a common-law right and in the absence of statutory provisions any one might not only issue his own notes for circulation but receive deposits as well.[1]

The states exercised no such power in connection with banking in our early history as they do today. The Bank of New York, which was one of the first American banks, asked for a charter in 1784 and being refused by the legislature it started business on June 9 of that year without any charter whatever. The only penalty, or rather disadvantage, was that the liability of the stockholders for the debts of the bank became unlimited. Finally, in 1791, after operating

---

[1] W. O. Scroggs, A Century of Banking Progress, p. 2.

six years without an authorization, the bank secured a charter. The charter contained a few limitations relating to the proportion to exist between capital and debts, holding of real estate, and trading in goods and securities.

The first half of the nineteenth century, as far as American banking is concerned, is a story of mismanagement, failures and fraud.[2] This was the period of the "Wildcat" banking in the South and West and "Free" banking in New York.[3] We find no really restrictive legislation upon banking at this time. On the contrary, it seemed as if the people as represented by their state governments had no rights against the banking institutions.

We search almost in vain through the law reports for any decisions on the rights or authority of the state over banks, or the duties of banks to the state. It may be said that no attempts were made to test or enforce the rights of the state against banks and that, as a matter of practice it had none. The banks were almost irresponsible.[4]

The greatest abuses were in connection with the lack of legislation upon the issue of bank notes which allowed unscrupulous persons to print and circulate worthless paper. Many banks were simply banks of issue without capital or with an insignificant reserve against enormous amounts of outstanding notes.[5] Legislatures in general made no important point of requiring reports from banks. During the first half of the century, banks guarded their affairs with

---

[2] "The writings of William Gouge and Condy Raguet, like the pages of Niles' *Register*, are filled with particular instances of downright fraud, and of reckless speculation which can hardly be distinguished from fraud, in the establishment, operation and closing of banks in the first half of the nineteenth century. . . . . Such misery was inflicted upon the country that some of the states in their constitutions entirely prohibited the existence of banks within their limits. Most commonly, however, the banking fraternity controlled the state governments." H. White, Money and Banking, p. 323.

[3] 16 of the 34 states had "Free" banking systems by 1860.

[4] Sumner, Banking, p. 352, quoted by White, *op. cit.*, p. 325.

[5] "The speculator comes to Indianapolis with a bundle of bank notes in one hand and the stock in the other; in twenty-four hours he is on his way to some distant point of the union to circulate what he denominates a legal currency, authorized by the legislature of Indiana. He has nominally located his bank in some remote part of the state, difficult of access, where he knows no banking facilities are required, and intends that his notes shall go into the hands of persons who will have no means of demanding redemption." The governor of Indiana in his message to the legislature in 1853, cited in "The Origin of the National Banking System," pp. 20–21.

secrecy, and it was difficult to obtain even the simplest information in regard to banking establishments.

Restrictive Legislation—Prohibiting Branches of Foreign Banks.—Such abuses provoked legislation to correct them. Massachusetts was the first state to place restrictions upon common-law banking by a law passed in 1799 forbidding any one to join an association to do banking unless authorized by law. By 1830 most of the states had confined the right of note issue to incorporated banks, and were starting to define just what powers a bank might exercise. Still later, legislation regarding reserves against deposits and requiring examination of and reports from banking concerns grew up.[6] After the passage of the National-Bank Act in 1864 the laws of the various states became more comprehensive and severe until today banking establishments are most minutely regulated for the protection of the public.

As this state banking legislation grew up, a principle interesting to this study was generally adopted and affirmed, namely, the prohibition against banks created outside of a state to operate within that state without special authorization and then under restrictions. One of the earliest to adopt this principle was the State of Pennsylvania which forbade in 1808 banks incorporated under the laws of other states or countries to do business within its boundaries.

These provisions of the laws of the various states of the union, which cause much comment abroad today because of the restrictions they place upon foreign banks wishing to establish branches in America, were not enacted because of a specific desire to legislate against the other nations of the world. They were adopted primarily because a state wished to protect its business enterprises against those of other states of the union.

---

[6] Regular yearly examinations were not authorized by a majority of the states until the last quarter of the nineteenth century, and yearly reports, not until after the American Civil War.

The Regulation of the Passive Function.—The two fundamental functions of a bank are those of borrowing and lending
credit, the collecting or borrowing of funds being called the
"passive" function and the lending of these funds, the "active."
It is chiefly the passive function which occasions special legislation with regard to branches of foreign banks. The state
may feel that it should guard the savings of its people and
prevent them from being deposited in branches of foreign
institutions which it does not regulate and which may be
unsound. It may also wish, if it is a new country where the
demand for capital is greater than the supply, to prevent the
country's savings from passing into foreigner's hands. In
the United States, foreign banks have been generally prohibited
from establishing branches to accept deposits from the public
because of the first reason. American banks have come to be
strictly regulated by the national and state governments with
the object of preventing loss to depositors whereas the banks
of foreign countries are not generally so regulated.

The Regulation of the Active Function.—The state may
regulate the active function of foreign banks, the lending of
capital within the state by foreign banks, if it feels that the
power thus gained by the foreign banks is too strong an influence upon the economic life of the country. Thus the
banking system of a new country may be regarded as an
"infant industry" and protection may be accorded it until
the native banks are judged to be strong enough to compete
successfully with foreign institutions. It is generally believed
that the statement of List,

The North American states were compelled to limit the importation of foreign manufactures and to protect their own industries.
That without these measures a manufacturing industry in the Atlantic
states could not have arisen is shown by their own experience and the
industrial history of other nations,[7]

---

[7] List, Das Nationale System der Politischen Oekonomie, pp. 192-3.

is open to the criticism that American industries would have arisen without protection and that protection only served to speed up their birth and growth. But in the case of American banking there seemed to be more strength in the argument for protection than in the case of American industry. Free trade in the latter case meant only that the United States would receive from abroad most of the manufactured articles consumed by the country until the day when its own industries would be able to furnish a substantial portion. On the other hand, the free trade principle applied to banking makes possible an actual invasion of the country by foreign establishments which come to stay and to compete with native establishments for the "control of the business of the nation." Taking into consideration the backwardness and inefficiency of American banking during the greater part of our history and the lack of American capital, it is possible that had foreign banks been allowed to establish branches throughout the United States, the banking institutions of such countries as England, France and Germany with their great experience and sound management would have come to exert an appreciable influence in the banking organization of the nation.[8] When once established this influence could not have been broken by the inexperienced American bankers unless restrictive legislation unfavorable to the established foreign banks were adopted. The international difficulties which would have arisen from such a procedure are evident.—So runs the argument for protection of the banking business of a country in the transition from new country to independent nation.

Protective Legislation Not Necessary.—Whatever may have been the value of the protectionist argument in the past, it has certainly lost its strength. Today, the United States

---

[8] See Brazil, p. 186 (footnote) and Argentina, p. 190. But the history of Canada suggests that the outcome might have been otherwise in the case of the United States.

is in a more advanced stage of economic development and it would seem that the banking organizations of New York and California at least are strong enough to look with equanimity upon the competition of foreign branch banks.

A review of the banking legislation of each one of the forty-eight states of the union is not necessary in an examination of the legal status of foreign banks in the United States. It is mainly in the State of New York that foreign banks wish to establish branches, and the fundamental provisions applying to foreign banks in New York are similar to those of the other states.

The Legal Status of Foreign Banks in New York

Branches of Foreign Banks Prohibited.—The legislation which governs all banks operating in New York, except national and federal reserve banks, is known as the Banking Law of 1914.[9] Under its provisions no banking institution created outside the State of New York may establish a branch bank within the state. Foreign banks are permitted to establish *agencies,* i.e., offices to engage in international banking operations, within the boundaries of New York State. These agencies are not branch banks for they are prohibited from accepting deposits in the United States, and many other powers possessed by a regular commercial banking establishment are denied them.

Restrictions Imposed on Foreign Agencies.—According to Article 3, section 145, of the Banking Law of New York the powers granted to agencies of foreign banks are as follows: buying, selling and collecting bills of exchange; issuing letters of credit; receiving money for transmission or transmitting it by draft, check, cable or otherwise; making sterling or

---

* The law "L. 1914 Ch. 369," passed April 16, 1914.

other loans. It will be noticed that the grant of powers is mute upon the subjects of deposits and note issue.

The acceptance of deposits and issuance of bank notes is expressly forbidden by Article 3, section 140, which holds that no foreign corporation other than a national bank or a federal reserve bank shall keep an office for the purpose of receiving deposits or making discounts or issuing notes or any other evidences of debt to be put into circulation as money unless expressly authorized to do so by law. Nor can the foreign agency transact the business of a savings and loan association as prohibited by Article 10, section 420.

Furthermore, Article 5, section 223, of the law prohibits the agencies of foreign banks from exercising the powers of receiving deposits of money or securities in trust and all other trust company powers stated in subdivisions 1, 4, 5, 6, 7 and 8 of section 185 (transfer or fiscal agent, trustee, guardian, etc.).

The agencies of foreign banks are also restricted in their powers to hold real estate in New York. Under Article 2, section 21 of the General Corporation Law of New York the agency may hold for five years any real property which it has secured through the foreclosure of a mortgage or by devise. Only agencies whose home offices are located in another state of the union or in Canada or Mexico may hold real property over five years. But if the states or countries mentioned do not accord similar privileges to New York corporations this right is not granted.[10]

Establishment of Agency by Foreign Bank.—Such are the rights and restrictions applying particularly to foreign banks in New York. We may now examine the formalities to be performed by a foreign bank in establishing and operating an agency in this state.

INSTALLATION.—Before opening an agency for business in

---

[10] Article 2, section 20 of the General Corporation Law of New York.

the State of New York, a foreign bank must obtain an authorization from the superintendent of banks in that state, and to secure this authorization the bank must :[11]

1. Be authorized by its charter to carry on a banking business abroad, and have complied with the laws of the state or country under which it is incorporated.

2. Submit an application certificate specifically stating: name; place in the state where business is to be transacted; name of agent through whom business is to be transacted; amount of capital subscribed for, and amount actually paid in; actual value of the assets of the corporation which must be at least $250,000 in excess of its liabilities; complete and detailed statement of its financial condition as of a date within sixty days prior to the date of application; duly exemplified copy of its charter, and verified copy of its by-laws or the equivalent thereof.

3. Designate to the superintendent of banks by a duly executed instrument in writing its true and lawful attorney upon whom a process or proceeding may be served with the same effect as if it were a domestic corporation. (This representative must be domiciled in the State of New York, and his residence is considered as the domicile of the foreign bank in New York.)

4. Pay to the superintendent of banks a license fee of $250.

Not until the foreign bank has fulfilled all the foregoing provisions to the satisfaction of the superintendent of banks may it begin business in the State of New York.[12]   The superintendent may reject applications for agencies which he feels would not be in the public interest.

OPERATION.—The agency of a foreign bank must renew its license each year, paying the renewal fee of $250 according to section 146 of the banking law.   It shall also, conforming to section 147, make written reports under oath in the form prescribed by the superintendent of banks showing the amount of its assets and liabilities and containing any other information

---

[11] Article 3, sections 144 and 145 of the Banking Law of New York.

[12] Foreign corporations authorized by their charter to do an investment business may establish agencies in New York by applying in the same general form as required of foreign commercial banks, but previous to beginning operations they must deposit $100,000 in American securities with the superintendent of banks (Article 8, sections 303–7).

requested by the superintendent. These reports are to be made whenever the superintendent so prescribes. At present regular reports are required from all banking establishments in New York every three months [13] in addition to such special reports as are prescribed. The superintendent also has power to inspect foreign bank agencies under Article 2, section 39, of the banking law, and regular inspections, in addition to special investigations, are made once each year.

A foreign bank agency in New York is governed by New York laws for public order and is subject to the courts of the state.[14] It may be declared in bankruptcy or closed by the superintendent of banks if he is convinced that it is violating the law or conducting its business in an unsafe manner.[15] Foreign bank agencies pay the same taxes as do American banks in New York.

The Effects of Restrictive Banking Legislation

Agencies of Foreign Banks in New York.—In considering the effects of the restrictive banking legislation of the State of New York mention will also be made of several other American states in which foreign banks have established agencies or branches. Although the banking law of New York prohibits offices of foreign banks from exercising in the state the fundamental functions of a commercial bank, a large number of foreign institutions have opened and maintained agencies in New York City. The foreign establishments feel that, even though such offices are restricted to foreign or international banking operations, they are better than dealing solely by correspondents. At the end of the year 1925 there were 33 agencies in New York of 32 foreign banks.

---

[13] Article 2, section 42 and Article 3, section 133.
[14] The foreign agency has the right to sue and be sued in the courts of New York just as if it were a New York corporation, and it is not required to deposit a "cautio judicatum solvi" or guarantee of costs (Article 2, section 28 of the Banking Law).
[15] Article 3, section 146; Article 2, sections 56–57.

The 33 New York agencies of foreign banks do a large business within the operations to which they are restricted and perform very useful services to their home countries. Yet the importance of foreign branch establishments in New York is very much less than it would be if restrictions were not placed on banking operations to be engaged in by foreign institutions.

Subsidiary Banks Created in New York by Foreign Banks. —Because the banking operations of an agency of a foreign bank are so limited by law other methods have been adopted by foreigners in search of freer banking operations in the United States. It has been possible for them to establish regular banking institutions in New York (and in other states) under the designation of state banks or state trust companies. In this way all restrictions against foreign banks are evaded and the bank or trust company so constituted stands upon a basis of equality with real American banks, but the nationality of its owners is foreign. This trend toward the creation of subsidiaries under New York laws has resulted in the establishment of six trust companies: the Anglo-South American Trust Company, the Banca Commerciale Italiana Trust Company, the Banco di Sicilia Trust Company, the Bank of Athens Trust Company, the Italian Discount and Trust Company, and the Trust Company of North America.[16] The foreign banks interested in these trust companies are respectively: the Anglo-South American Bank, Ltd., (England), the Banca Commerciale Italiana (Italy), the Banco di Sicilia (Italy), the Banque d'Athènes (Greece), the Banca Italiana di Sconto (Italy), and the Banco Nacional Ultramarino (Portugal).

Branches of Foreign Banks Prohibited in California.— Section 7 of the California Bank Act states:

[16] Incorporated investment banks in New York controlled by foreign banks are the French American Banking Corporation and the J. Henry Schroeder Banking Corporation. They are not permitted to accept deposits. Foreign private investment banks may establish branch houses in New York without restrictions. Huth and Company in New York City, a branch of Frederick Huth and Company of London, is an example.

. . . a foreign banking corporation shall not be permitted to accept deposits of money in this state but may receive a certificate from the superintendent of banks to transact in this state only the business of buying or selling, paying or collecting bills of exchange, or of issuing letters of credit, or of receiving money for transmission, or transmitting the same by draft, check, cable, or otherwise, or of making loans.

. . . those foreign banking corporations that now have power to do a banking business in this state and which now receive deposits of money shall be permitted to continue to accept money on deposit.

The California Bank Act has since 1917 prohibited offices in California of foreign banks from accepting deposits, but the two branches at San Francisco of the Yokohama Specie Bank, Ltd. (Japan), and the Canadian Bank of Commerce (Canada), established prior to 1917, continued to accept deposits. The agencies in California of foreign banks are: the Los Angeles office of the Yokohama Specie Bank, Ltd., and the San Francisco offices of the Hongkong and Shanghai Banking Corporation (China), the Bank of Montreal (Canada), the Sumitomo Bank, Ltd., (Japan), the Commercial Bank of Spanish America, Ltd., (England), and the Bank of Canton, Ltd., (China).

The state banks in California which are owned or controlled by foreign banks are: the British American Bank, San Francisco, owned by the Bank of Montreal, Canada; the Canton Bank, San Francisco, controlled by the Oriental Commercial Bank, Ltd., of Hongkong, China; the Sumitomo Bank of California, Sacramento, owned by the Sumitomo Bank, Ltd., of Osaka, Japan.

Subsidiaries of Foreign Banks in Other States.—In the State of Washington the Canadian Bank of Commerce and the Sumitomo Bank at Seattle are institutions created under the laws of the state and are owned by foreign capital for the most part. They are permitted to accept deposits and do a general banking but not a trust business. In Illinois at Chicago the branches of the Bank of Montreal and the Bank of Nova Scotia, which were established before the passage of the present banking law in 1920, do a regular banking business, and in Massachusetts at Boston the branch of the Bank of Nova Scotia, established before the enactment of the present banking law which demands annual examination of a foreign bank opening and maintaining a branch bank in the Commonwealth, is engaged in a regular banking business. Foreign branch bank establishment is now extremely impracticable in Massachusetts due to the expenses of examination which are chargeable to the foreign bank examined.[17]

Although the banking laws of our states prohibit or hinder the establishment of bona fide branches of foreign banks, yet foreign banks are able to secure the rights and privileges denied them by securing interests in important banks, which appear to be purely American to the outsider, or by creating subsidiaries under state laws.

Foreign banks find it profitable to have establishments fully empowered to carry on all banking operations in certain American cities, just as in all the world financial centers, and when one method of procedure is closed to them they adopt another.

---

[17] Section 38 of General Laws, Chapter 167. Branches of foreign banks may accept deposits and there are no expressed restrictions on their activities (sections 37 to 45) but no branches of foreign banks have been established since the passage of the law.

CHAPTER XIII

THE QUESTION OF RECIPROCITY

Better American Foreign Banking Facilities.—Today, due to the establishment of a discount market at New York supported by the federal reserve banks, the development of American bankers' acceptances, the growth of foreign departments in our banks, the rise of acceptance houses and corporations for foreign financial operations, and the establishment of offices abroad by our banking institutions, American foreign trade has adequate American foreign banking facilities for the first time in history and it is better promoted than at any time in the past.

Few Legal Obstacles Encountered Abroad.—In their expansion abroad American banks have generally met with no restrictions and in most countries where they have branches they operate upon a basis of equality with the native institutions. Canada, where branches of foreign banks are prohibited, and Russia, where the conditions surrounding the establishment of foreign enterprises are as yet unsettled and unsatisfactory, are perhaps the only countries in which American banks might wish to establish branches and are held back from so doing. Had our banks in their foreign expansion encountered such legal restrictions as are now imposed by our laws on foreign banks wishing to operate in the United States there would be no American foreign branch banking system today. Here arises a question that is becoming more and more important: what is to be the attitude of the United States toward foreign banks?

Attitude To Take Toward Foreign Banks.—At present, in return for the freedom to install and operate branches granted by foreign nations to our banks, we offer restrictions. No foreign bank may establish a fully empowered branch bank in either New York or California—the states where the possession of banking establishments is most advantageous to foreign banks. Foreign banks may indeed establish subsidiaries or commandites in these states, but, as pointed out in the chapter on methods of foreign banking contact and as indicated in the present foreign banking organizations of the great banks of the world, the branch bank is generally preferred to these two other forms of banking expansion for transacting foreign operations. It would seem only just that if a nation permits its banks to take advantage of the welcome of certain foreign countries which treat these banks equally with their own native establishments, the nation in question should not place the banks of such countries at a disadvantage in competing in its territory with its domestic banking institutions. This is reciprocity, and if the countries in which our banks are now established should pass laws restricting the establishment and operation of our banks similar to the laws obtaining for their banks in certain American states, the procedure would be essentially just.

The Question of Reciprocity.—There were discussions in favor of applying such a system of reciprocity to foreign banks by European nations and by some South American countries during and after the World War. Various motives prevented its application. In certain foreign centers, notably London, Paris, and Berlin, the presence of foreign banks is regarded with approval as these banks contribute to the development of trade and commerce, supply capital for the market, and provide an outlet for the investment of the excess capital of the country. The fact that New York has not been able to compete with London as a financial center is generally agreed to be due to the restrictive legislation which hinders foreign banks from operating freely in New York.[1] A number of nations, observing the invasion of their territories by American banks and realizing the position of their banks in the United States, felt very keenly the injustice of the situation and only refrained from enforcing a régime of reciprocity against American banks because they did not feel in a position after the war to enter upon a policy which would without doubt have resulted in international antagonism.

The International Chamber of Commerce has endeavored to bring the nations together upon a harmonious policy concerning foreign branch banks, and declared at its first congress in London in 1921:

Whereas it is contrary to the interests of international trade and to good understanding between nations that restrictive laws or special taxes be imposed by a country upon the foreign banks established in its territory in addition to those to which the native banks are already subject, or that measures of favor be exclusively accorded to native banks; the Congress demands urgently of all countries in which the present legislation contains restrictive measures or special treatments to take the initiative to abolish these laws, if not in every case, at least for the benefit of those foreign countries which accord reciprocity.[2]

Attitude of American Great Banks.—The above declaration voices the feeling of most of the nations of the world. In this country the people are in favor of prohibiting or restricting branch banking by foreign establishments while the great banks of the United States, on the contrary, have been becoming more in favor of according equality of treatment to foreign banks. Fred I. Kent, vice-president of the Bankers Trust Company, gave the attitude of the great New York banks before the first congress of the International Chamber of Commerce:

The branches of foreign banks contribute to increase the business of a country much more than they tend to monopolize it, and the

---

[1] Marcus Wallenberg, League of Nations Document, E.F.S. 80. A 46, p. 4.
[2] Traitement des Banques Etrangères, p. 5.

primordial situation of England in the world is in great part due to the fact that she opens her doors to foreign commerce of all parts of the world and to the fact that she encourages it in every manner.

The restrictive measures against foreign institutions which exist in the State of New York work against the interests of this state. . . . A profound study of foreign banks shows that branches of foreign banks established in a country bring in much more business than they take away from the citizens of the country.

Thus the countries which have very liberal laws for the establishment of foreign branch banks draw the greatest profits from these laws; the restrictive measures established by the laws of the different states of the United States are more contrary to the interests of these states in general than they are to the interests of the citizens of other countries.

Legal Measures to Allow Branches of Foreign Banks.— In the New York legislature efforts have been made to modify the law concerning branches of foreign banks. In 1920, the Cotillo bill was passed but vetoed by the governor. Another bill, No. 2305, was introduced on April 17, 1923 but after being passed by the House was rejected by the Senate. This bill would have allowed foreign banks to establish branches in cities of 1,000,000 population or over for the purpose of:

. . . discounting and negotiating notes, drafts, bills of exchange and other evidences of debt, or of receiving deposits, or buying and selling exchange, coin or bullion, or of lending money on real or personal security or any part of such business.

Only a foreign bank having a combined capital and surplus of at least $1,000,000 and assets of at least $1,000,000 in excess of its liabilities, the sums being based upon the current rate of exchange at the time of application for license, might take advantage of this privilege. The bank would also have to deposit stocks and bonds with the superintendent of banks as a pledge of good faith, and maintain a reserve of 18 per cent against the demand deposits of the branch. Separate books and records would be kept for the branch and the bank, in respect to its branch, would be subject to all the provisions of the banking law in relation to examinations by the superintendent of banks and to reports on the business transacted in the State of New York. The bill also included a "reciprocal provision" to the effect that the superintendent of banks might refuse a license to a bank of a foreign country not according privileges substantially equivalent to those accorded by the bill to foreign banks.

The opposition to the bills seeking to ameliorate the condition of agencies of foreign banks in New York seems to come primarily from the numerous small bankers who fear an invasion of great foreign banks. The movement for the passage of such bills has not ceased and the question remains to be settled definitively. It would seem that the banking organizations of New York and California are strongly enough developed to look with composure upon the competition of fully empowered branches of foreign banks, especially if such branches were limited to the cities of New York, San Francisco, and Los Angeles. And as far as the safeguarding of the interests of American depositors is concerned, the branches of foreign banks may be so regulated and supervised as to leave no greater risk of loss than is present in the case of the American banking establishments.

Question Unsettled.—Foreign nations are desirous that their banks receive equality of treatment in the United States, and most foreign countries now have provisions in their laws calling upon the minister of finances or another official to examine the legal status of their banks in the country of the bank applying for permission to establish a branch, and to prohibit establishment or to grant permission with or without restrictions as may be fit. Here is a power that may be used to the great inconvenience of our foreign branch banks. That it has not been employed in the past offers no proof that it will not be used in the future, although foreign nations would naturally hesitate to take advantage of it. Thus the question concerning the American attitude toward foreign banks is due to press more and more for decision in the future, and it should ultimately result in a declaration for equal treatment of foreign branch banks with our own domestic establishments.

APPENDIX

Table I. The Foreign Expansion of American Banks

The table shows the number of regular foreign branches possessed by American incorporated commercial banking institutions on December 31, 1913, on December 31, 1920, and on June 30, 1926, and indicates the number of branches established, acquired, and transferred.*

	1913	1920	1926	Estab.	Acq.	Transf.
AMERICAN BANKS AND SUBSIDIARIES:						
1. Jarvis-Conklin Mortgage Trust Company				1		1
2. North American Trust Company					1	1
3. Equitable Trust Company	2	2	4	3	1	
Equitable Eastern Banking Corporation			2	2		
4. Guaranty Trust Company	1	7	8	9		
5. Farmers' Loan and Trust Company	2	2	1	2		1
6. Empire Trust Company	1	1	1	1		
7. National City Bank		57	51	64	10	3
International Banking Corporation	16	29	22	36	2	9
National City Bank (France)			1		1	
Bank of Haiti		10	10			
8. Commercial National Bank				2		2
9. First National Bank of Boston		1	2	2		
10. Bankers Trust Company		1	2	2		
11. Chase National Bank			3	3		
Total	22	100	107	134		3
AMERICAN FOREIGN BANKING CORPORATIONS:						
1. Continental Banking and Trust Company	4	4		4		
2. Mercantile Bank of the Americas		45		45		23
3. American Foreign Banking Corporation		19		17	2	3
4. Asia Banking Corporation		9		11		
5. Park-Union Foreign Banking Corporation		4		4		
6. Bank of Central and South America						23
Total		81		81		
GRAND TOTAL	26	181	107	215		

* The American Express Company, Inc., (see p. 160) had 38 foreign branches in 1920 and 47 in 1926.

TABLE 2. THE GEOGRAPHICAL DISTRIBUTION OF AMERICAN FOREIGN
BRANCH BANKS

The table shows the location, according to countries, of the foreign
branches of American banks and subsidiaries and of the foreign branches
of the American Express Company, Inc., on June 30, 1926.

Foreign Branches of American Banks and Subsidiaries	Foreign Branches of the American Express Company, Inc.
EUROPE	EUROPE
Belgium 6	Belgium 3
England 10	Denmark 1
France 5	France 5
Italy 2	Germany 3
Spain 2	Great Britain 8
― 25	Greece 2
	Holland 2
LATIN AMERICA	Italy 4
Argentina 3	Monaco 1
Brazil 4	Switzerland 3
Chile 2	― 32
Cuba 26	
Haiti 10	LATIN AMERICA
Mexico 1	Argentina 1
Panama 4	NEAR EAST
Peru 1	Egypt 1
Porto Rico 1	Palestine 1
Santo Domingo 7	Turkey 2
Uruguay 1	― 4
Venezuela 1	
― 61	FAR EAST
	Ceylon 1
FAR EAST	China 4
China 10	India 2
India 3	Japan 1
Japan 4	Philippines 1
Java 1	Straits Settlements 1
Philippines 2	― 10
Straits Settlements 1	
― 21	
World Total 107	World Total 47

TABLE 3. AGENCIES IN NEW YORK OF FOREIGN BANKS ON
DECEMBER 31, 1925

NAME OF BANK	HOME ADDRESS OF BANK
1. Banque Belge Pour l'Etranger	Brussels, Belgium
2. Anglo-South American Bank, Ltd.	London, England
3. Bank of London and South America, Ltd.	" "
4. Barclay's Bank, Ltd.	" "
5. Chartered Bank of India, Australia, and China	" "
6. Commercial Bank of Spanish America, Ltd.	" "
7. Mercantile Bank of India, Ltd.	" "
8. Standard Bank of South Africa, Ltd.	" "
9. Bank of Montreal	Montreal, Quebec
10. Bank of Nova Scotia	Halifax, Nova Scotia
11. Canadian Bank of Commerce	Toronto, Ontario
12. Dominion Bank	" "
13. Royal Bank of Canada	Montreal, Quebec
14. Bank of Canton, Ltd.	Hongkong, China
15. Hongkong and Shanghai Banking Corporation	" "
16. Bank of Athens	Athens, Greece
17. National Bank of Greece	" "
18. Banca Commerciale Italiana	Milan, Italy
19. Banco Di Napoli *	Naples, Italy
20. Banco Di Roma	Rome, Italy
21. Credito Italiano	Genoa and Milan, Italy
22. Instituto Italiano di Credito Maritimo	Rome, Italy
23. Bank of Chosen	Seoul (Korea), Japan
24. Bank of Taiwan, Ltd.	Taipeh, Japan
25. Mitsubishi Bank, Ltd.	Tokio, Japan
26. Mitsui Bank, Ltd.	" "
27. Sumitomo Bank, Ltd.	Osaka, Japan
28. Yokohama Specie Bank, Ltd.	Yokahama, Japan
29. Philippine National Bank	Manila, P. I.
30. Union Bank of the Co-operative Societies of Poland	Posen, Poland
31. Banca Chrissoveloni, Societate Anonima Romana	Bucharest, Roumania
32. National Bank of South Africa, Ltd.	Pretoria, Union of South Africa

*Two agencies at New York.

BIBLIOGRAPHY

Agger, E. E. Organized Banking. New York, Henry Holt & Co., 1918.

Anderson, B. M., Jr. Effects of the War on Money, Credit, and Banking in France and the United States. New York, Oxford University Press, 1919.

Angell, Theory of International Prices, Cambridge, 1926, Harvard.

Bankers Magazine. New York, Bankers Publishing Co.

Barazzetti, P. Régime des Banques Etrangères dans les Principales Législations. Paris, Rousseau, 1923.

Beckhart, B. H. Discount Policy of the Federal Reserve System. New York, Henry Holt & Co., 1924.

Berrogain. Expansion du Commerce Extérieur. Paris, Delagrave, 1916.

Bishop, A. L. Outlines of American Foreign Commerce. Boston, Ginn & Co., 1923.

Boggs, T. H. International Trade Balance in Theory and Practice. New York, Macmillan Co., 1922.

Chicago Banker, Chicago.

Clunet. Journal du Droit International Privé, Paris.

Combining for Export Trade. New York, Guaranty Trust Co., 1920.

Commerce and Finance, New York.

Commercial and Financial Chronicle, New York.

Cook, A. B. Financing Exports and Imports. New York, The Ronald Press Company, 1923.

Co-operation in American Export Trade. Washington, Federal Trade Commission, 1916.

Course in Foreign Trade. New York, Business Training Corporation, 1916.

Culbertson, W. S. Commercial Policy in Wartime and After. New York, D. Appleton & Co., 1919.

Dufourcq-Lagelouse, L. Banques Etrangères en France. Paris, Dalloz, 1922.

Eckardt, H. M. P. A Rational Banking System. New York, Harper & Bros., 1911.

Edwards, G. W. International Trade Finance. New York, Henry Holt & Co., 1924.

Federal Reserve Bank of New York Reports, New York.

Federal Reserve Board Reports, Washington.

Federal Reserve Bulletins and Circulars, Washington.

Federal Trade Commission Reports, Washington.

Filsinger, E. B. Exporting to Latin America. New York, D. Appleton & Co., 1919.

Ford, L. and T. Foreign Trade of the United States. New York, Chas. Scribner's Sons, 1920.

Greenwood, E. Industrial Digest, New York.

Hough, B. O. Practical Exporting. New York, Johnson Export Publishing Co., 1915.

Houpin et Bosvieux. Traité Général des Sociétés. Paris, Sirey, 1918.

Hull, W. H. Practical Problems in Banking and Currency. New York, Macmillan Co., 1907.

Jacobs. Bank Acceptances. Washington, National Monetary Commission Report, 1910.

Journal of Commerce, New York.

Journal of the American Bankers Association, New York.

Kemmerer, E. W. A. B. C. of the Federal Reserve System. Princeton University Press, 4th ed., 1920.

Kidd, H. C. Kidd on Foreign Trade. New York, Prentice-Hall, 1921.

Kniffin, W. H., Jr. Practical Work of a Bank. New York, Bankers Publishing Co., 1916.

——Commercial Paper. New York, Bankers Publishing Co., 1924.

Lahee, A. W. Our Competitors and Markets. New York, Henry Holt & Co., 1924.

Langston, L. H. Practical Bank Operation. New York, The Ronald Press Company, 1921.

Laughlin, J. L. Banking Progress. New York, Chas. Scribner's Sons, 1920.

List, F. Das Nationale System der Politischen Oekonomie. Jena, Fischer, 4th ed., 1922.

Litman, S. Essentials of International Trade. New York, John Wiley & Son, 1923.

Loeb, C. G. Legal Status of American Corporations in France. Paris, Lecram, 1921.

Magee, J. D. Materials for the Study of Banking. New York, Prentice-Hall, 1923.

Moulton, H. G. Financial Organization. Chicago, University of Chicago Press, 1921.

National Foreign Trade Convention Reports. New York, National Foreign Trade Council.

Origin of the National Banking System. Washington, National Monetary Commission Report, 1910.

Pepper, C. M. American Foreign Trade. New York, Century Co., 1919.

Phelps, C. W. Banques Américaines à l'Etranger et Principalement en France. Paris, Dalloz, 1924.

Preciado, A. A. Exporting to the World. New York, James A. McCann, 1920.

Reed, H. L. Development of Federal Reserve Policy. Boston, Houghton Mifflin, 1922.

Riesser. Die Deutschen Grossbanken und ihre Konzentration in Zusammenhang mit der Entwicklung des Gesamtwirtschaft in Deutschland. Jena, 4th ed., 1912.

Robinson, L. R. Foreign Credit Facilities in the United Kingdom. New York, Columbia University Press, 1923.

——Investment Trust Organization and Management. New York. The Ronald Press Company, 1926.

Scroggs, W. O. Century of Banking Progress. New York, Doubleday Page & Co., 1924.

Secretary of the Treasury's Reports, Washington.

Spalding, W. F. Foreign Exchange and Foreign Bills. London, G. P. Putnam's Sons, 1919.

Speaker, L. M. Investment Trust. Chicago, A. W. Shaw, 1924.

Special Agents Series. Washington, Department of Commerce.

Statistical Abstract of the United States, Washington.

Subercaseaux, G. Monetary and Banking Policy of Chile. London, Oxford University Press, 1922.

Trade Information Bulletins. Washington, Department of Commerce.

Traitement des Banques Etrangères. Paris, International Chamber of Commerce, 1921.

Veyrièras. Sociétés Etrangères en France. Saumur, France, Roland, 1921.

Viner, Jacob. Canada's Balance of International Indebtedness. (Harvard Economic Studies, Vol. 26.) Cambridge, Mass., Harvard University Press, 1924.

Wall Street Journal, New York.

Wallenberg, M. Reciprocal Treatment of Branches of Foreign Banks in Different Countries. League of Nations Document E. F. S. 80 A. 46, Boston, World Peace Foundation.

White, H. Money and Banking. Boston, Ginn & Co., 5th ed., 1911.

Willis, H. P. American Banking. New York, Henry Holt & Co., 1918.
——Federal Reserve System. New York, The Ronald Press Company, 1923.
Young, Edward Hilton. Foreign Companies and Other Corporations. New York, G. P. Putnam's Sons, 1912.

INDEX